Complicated Kris Northern

"This image illustrates some of the best qualities of fractals—infinity, reiteration, and self similarity."– **Kris Northern**

Investigations

IN NUMBER, DATA, AND SPACE®

Glenview, Illinois • Boston, Massachusetts
Chandler, Arizona • Upper Saddle River, New Jersey

The Investigations curriculum was developed by TERC, Cambridge, MA.

This material is based on work supported by the National Science Foundation ("NSF") under Grant No.ESI-0095450. Any opinions, findings, and conclusions or recommendations expressed in this material are those of the author(s) and do not necessarily reflect the views of the National Science Foundation.

ISBN-13: 978-0-328-69753-3

ISBN-10: 0-328-69753-2

2 3 4 5 6 7 8 9 10 V011 15 14 13 12 11

Complicated Kris Northern

"This image illustrates some of the best qualities of fractals—infinity, reiteration, and self similarity."– **Kris Northern**

Investigations
IN NUMBER, DATA, AND SPACE®

Counting, Coins, and Combinations

Using 10 Cubes

Use 10 cubes to make two things.
Draw what you make, and use
numbers to describe them.
Here is an example.

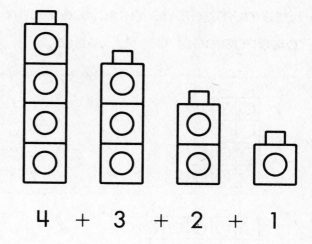

4 + 3 + 2 + 1

1. Draw what you made. Use numbers to
describe it.

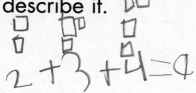

2 + 3 + 4 = 9

2. Draw what you made. Use numbers to
describe it.

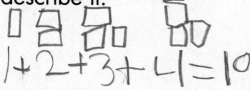

1 + 2 + 3 + 4 = 10

10 Cubes

Use numbers to describe each
arrangement of 10 cubes.

NOTE Students use combinations
of numbers that equal 10.

SMH 46

1.

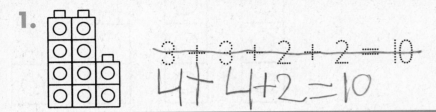

$3 + 3 + 2 + 2 = 10$

$4 + 4 + 2 = 10$

2.

$4 + 3 + 2 = 9$ 8

3.

$2 + 4 + 4 = 10$

4.

$2 + 3 + 5 = 10$

5.

$3 + 3 + 4 = 11$

6.

$3 + 3 + 2 = 8$

Cover and Count: Shape A

Use pattern blocks to cover Shape A in different ways. Record the number of blocks in the chart.

	Yellow hexagons	Red trapezoids	Blue rhombuses	Orange squares	Tan thin rhombuses	Green triangles	Total blocks
1st way	0	2	2	0	0	6	4
2nd way	0	0	2	0	0	6	8
3rd way	0	1	3	0	0	0	5
4th way	0	1	3	0	0	1	5
5th way	0	0	3	0	0	4	

Cover and Count: Shape B

Use pattern blocks to cover Shape B in different ways. Record the number of blocks in the chart.

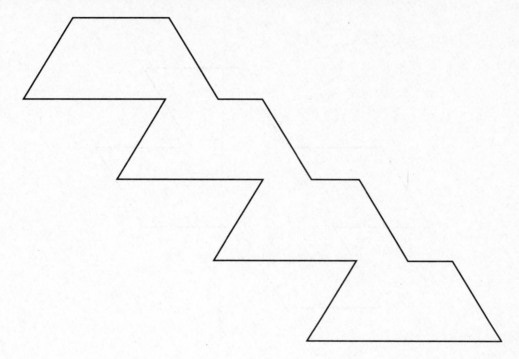

	Yellow hexagons	Red trapezoids	Blue rhombuses	Orange squares	Tan thin rhombuses	Green triangles	Total blocks
1st way	0	2	1	0	0	4	4
2nd way	0	1	2	0	0	5	3
3rd way	0	1	2	0	0	5	2
4th way	0	2	2	0	0	2	5
5th way	0	2	2	0	0	2	0

Cover and Count: Shape C

Use pattern blocks to cover Shape C in different ways. Record the number of blocks in the chart.

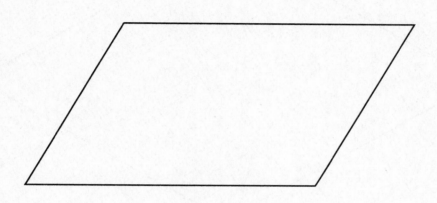

	Yellow hexagons	Red trapezoids	Blue rhombuses	Orange squares	Tan thin rhombuses	Green triangles	Total blocks
1st way	0	2	2	0	0	1	4
2nd way	1	0	2	0	0	2	1
3rd way	1	1	1	0	0	1	2
4th way	0	1	3	0	0	3	3
5th way	1	1	0	0	0	3	0

Cover and Count: Shape D

Use pattern blocks to cover Shape D in different ways. Record the number of blocks in the chart.

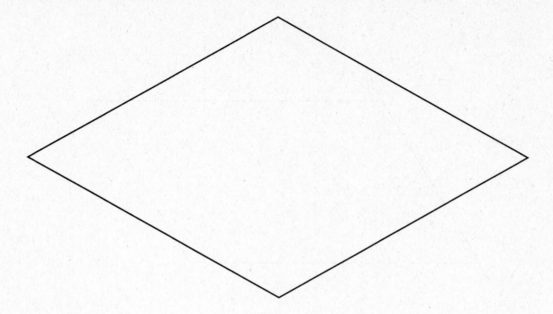

	Yellow hexagons	Red trapezoids	Blue rhombuses	Orange squares	Tan thin rhombuses	Green triangles	Total blocks
1st way							
2nd way							
3rd way							
4th way							
5th way							

Cover and Count: Shape E

Use pattern blocks to cover Shape E in different ways. Record the number of blocks in the chart.

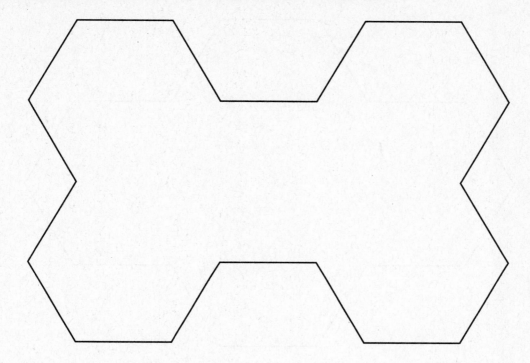

	Yellow hexagons	Red trapezoids	Blue rhombuses	Orange squares	Tan thin rhombuses	Green triangles	Total blocks
1st way							
2nd way							
3rd way							
4th way							
5th way							

Cover and Count: Shape F

Use pattern blocks to cover Shape F in different ways. Record the number of blocks in the chart.

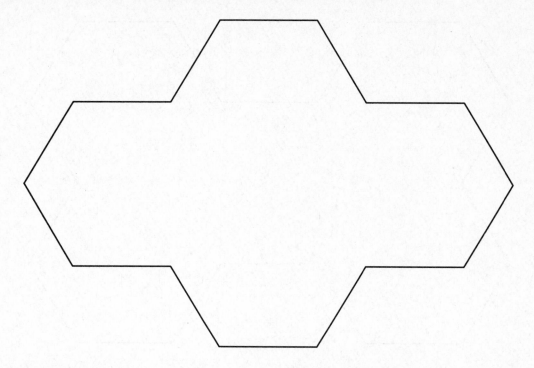

	Yellow hexagons	Red trapezoids	Blue rhombuses	Orange squares	Tan thin rhombuses	Green triangles	Total blocks
1st way							
2nd way							
3rd way							
4th way							
5th way							

Shape Pictures

Jake and Sally are making designs with pattern blocks.

NOTE Students answer questions about designs made from pattern blocks.

SMH **99**

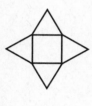

A triangle has 3 sides and 3 corners.

A square has 4 sides and 4 corners.

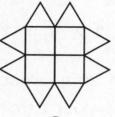

A   **B**   **C**   **D**

1. Which design has the most triangles? _____

2. Which design has the most squares? _____

3. Which design uses only triangles? _____

4. Which design uses only 1 square? _____

Ongoing Review

5. Which number combination does **not** make 10?

(A) 5 + 5

(B) 5 + 4 + 1

(C) 6 + 3

(D) 2 + 2 + 2 + 2 + 2

Arranging 10 Objects

Find 10 objects that are small enough to move around, such as rocks, pennies, or buttons. Group them in different ways. Record at least two of the ways and use numbers to describe them.

NOTE Students find combinations of numbers that equal 10. There are many possible solutions.

 46

Example:

$$4 + 3 + 2 + 1 = 10$$

1. Show how you grouped your objects.
Use numbers to describe your arrangement.

2. Show how you grouped your objects.
Use numbers to describe your arrangement.

Session 1.2

Counting, Coins, and Combinations

> **NOTE** Students use clues to solve number riddles.
>
> **SMH** 24

Number Riddles

Use the clues to guess these numbers.

1. I am the number of hours in the day.

I am what you get if you add 12 + 12.

I am 2 tens and 4 ones.

What number am I? ___24___

2. I am the number of senses you have.

I am one greater than four.

I am one less than six.

What number am I? ___5___

3. I am the number of states in the U.S.A.

I am half of 100.

I am 10 greater than 40.

What number am I? ___5___

Ongoing Review

4. Which pair of cards has a total greater than 12?

A   5 6

B   4 8

C   3 9

D   6 7

Clocks

NOTE Students practice telling time to the hour.

 134

1. Read each clock and write the time.

2. What is the same about all of these clocks?
Why? (Hint: Look at the big hand.) Write your
answer on another sheet of paper.

Today's Number: 7

Today's Number is _7_ .

5 + 2

5 + 1 + 1

10 − 3

Show different ways to make Today's Number.

$6 + 1 = 7$ $7 + 0 = 7$ $4 + 2 = 7$

$8 - 1 = 7$ $30 - 23 = 7$

$20 - 13 = 7$ $0 + 7 = 7$ $9 - 2 = 7$

$7 + 0 = 7$ $15 - 8 = 7$ 1

$11 + 4 = 7$ $13 - 6 = 7$ $+$

$19 - 12 = 7$ 6

$= 7$

Using the 100 Chart

Solve these problems.
Fill in the totals on the 100 chart.

NOTE Students practice +1 and +2 addition combinations and sequencing numbers 1–100.

SMH 24, 44, 45

1. $1 + 7 =$ __8__

2. $2 + 3 =$ __5__

3. $9 + 2 =$ __11__

4. $8 + 1 =$ __9__

5. $4 + 1 =$ __5__

6. $2 + 5 =$ __7__

7. $7 + 2 =$ __9__

8. $1 + 6 =$ __7__

9. Fill in all of the other numbers on the 100 chart.

1	2	3	4	5	6	7	8	9	10
11	12	13	14	15	16	17	18	19	20
21	22	23	24	25	26	27	28	29	30
31	32	33	34	35	36	37	38	39	40
41	42	43	44	45	46	47	48	49	50
51	52	53	54	55	56	57	58	59	60
61	62	63	64	65	66	67	68	69	70
71	72	73	74	75	76	77	78	79	80
81	82	83	84	85	86	87	88	89	90
91	92	93	94	95	96	97	98	99	100

Enough for the Class?

1. There are _____ children in our class.

2. I counted the cubes in Bag _____.

3. How many cubes are there altogether? _____

4. Are there enough for the class?   YES   NO

5. Were there any extra cubes?   YES   NO

How many? _____

6. Do you need more cubes?   YES   NO

How many? _____

7. How did you figure it out? Show your work.

Give Me 5!

NOTE Students write addition and subtraction expressions that equal 5. There are many possible solutions.

 55

1. Find as many ways as you can to make 5.

By adding numbers

1 + 3 + 1

4 + 1

By subtracting numbers

6 – 1

5 – 0

Ongoing Review

2. Which number is 5 more than 12?

(A) 7　　(B) 15　　(C) 17　　(D) 23

Identifying Coins

Look carefully at each coin. Record what you notice.

1.

A **penny** is worth _____ ¢.

2.

A **nickel** is worth _____ ¢.

3.

A **dime** is worth _____ ¢.

4.

A **quarter** is worth

_____ ¢.

Are There Enough?

Ms. Bank has 25 pencils.
There are 18 students in
Ms. Bank's class.

NOTE Students determine whether there are enough items for each child. Then they figure out how many are left over, or how many more are needed.

1. Are there enough for the class?   YES   NO

2. Are there any extra pencils?   YES   NO

How many? _____

3. Does Ms. Bank need more pencils?   YES   NO

How many? _____

4. How did you figure it out? Show your work.

Enough for the Picnic?

NOTE Students practice comparing 2 two-digit numbers.

24 people are coming to your house for a picnic. There are 30 sandwiches in your picnic basket.

1. Will there be enough sandwiches? _____

2. Will there be any leftovers? _____

3. If so, how many? _____

Use this space to show your work.

Ongoing Review

4. How many more rainy days than sunny days does the graph show?

Ⓐ 3 more

Ⓑ 2 more

Ⓒ 1 more

Ⓓ 0 more

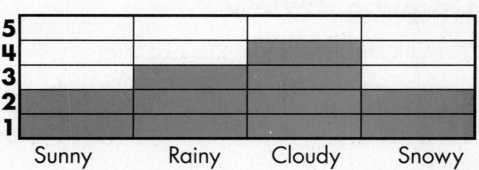

The Weather

Trading Coins

1. Draw a line to show equal trades for each group of coins.

NOTE Students practice counting money and finding coin equivalencies.

SMH 20

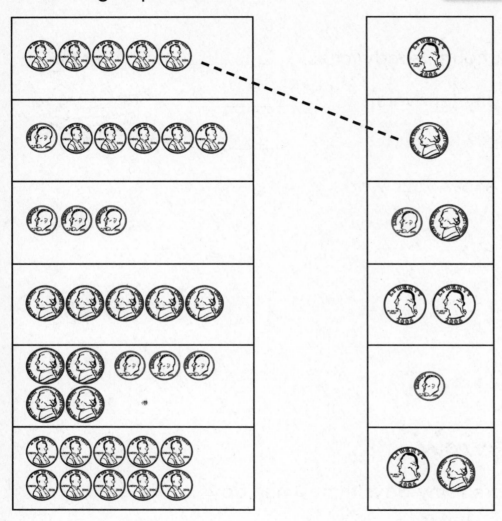

Ongoing Review

2. Mark the statement that is **not** true.

(A) $6 + 4 = 10$ (C) $10 - 4 = 6$

(B) $4 + 6 = 10$ (D) $10 - 6 = 3$

Our First Pocket Day

Write about our first Pocket Day.
Think about these questions as you write.

- What was the question we were trying to answer?

- What did we do? What tools did we use?

- What did we find out? How many pockets were there?

_____

_____

_____

_____

_____

_____

_____

Name

Counting, Coins, and Combinations

Date

Daily Practice

Coins

How many pennies are these coins worth?

NOTE Students review the value of coins.

SMH 19, 20

1.

2.

3.

4.

Pockets at Home

Tell your family about Pocket Day.

Find out how many pockets each person is wearing. Then, figure out how many pockets your family is wearing altogether. You can guess first.

If you need more space, use the back of this page.

> **NOTE** Students collect and record data about how many pockets people are wearing. They combine several numbers to find out the total number of pockets.

Person	Number of Pockets

My family is wearing _____ pockets altogether.
Here is how I figured it out.

What Went Wrong?

Here are parts of 3 counting strips.
Try to find what went wrong.
Correct the mistakes.

NOTE Students practice counting and sequencing numbers.

SMH 26

1.

17
18
19
20
30
40

2.

21
22
23
23
24
25

3.

97
98
99
100
200
300

Ongoing Review

4. What is the value of 1 penny, 2 nickels, and 3 dimes?

(A) 6¢   (B) 26¢   (C) 41¢   (D) 51¢

Daily Practice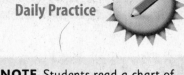

Pocket Day

1. Read the chart.

Then draw pockets on the students.

> **NOTE** Students read a chart of a set of data. They add together several numbers to find the total number of pockets.
>
> **SMH** 94–95

Pockets	Students
0	1
1	3
2	2

2. Record the total number of pockets here: _____

Today's Number: 9

Today's Number is 9 .

5 + 4

5 + 2 + 2

10 − 1

Show different ways to make Today's Number.

NOTE Students write addition and subtraction expressions that are equal to Today's Number.

SMH 55

Make 10

Circle the two cards that make 10.

NOTE Students practice finding combinations that make 10.

SMH 46

1.   6   3   4   8

2.   1   2   8   7

3.   6   5   3   5

4.   2   9   7   3

Ongoing Review

5. How many children were surveyed?

Do You Have a Cat?

Yes	No
‖‖‖ ‖‖‖	‖‖‖ ‖‖‖ ‖‖‖

(A) 24   (B) 25   (C) 30   (D) 42

The Sum Is . . .

Circle the two cards that make each sum.

NOTE Students find addition combinations that equal a given sum.

SMH 43

1. The sum is 15.

| 5 | 3 | 10 |

2. The sum is 9.

| 6 | 4 | 5 |

3. The sum is 16.

| 8 | 8 | 7 |

4. The sum is 7.

| 5 | 3 | 2 |

5. The sum is 11.

| 9 | 1 | 10 |

6. The sum is 13.

| 6 | 2 | 7 |

7. The sum is 4.

| 3 | 2 | 2 |

8. The sum is 20.

| 10 | 9 | 10 |

Ongoing Review

9. How many cubes are in the cube trains?

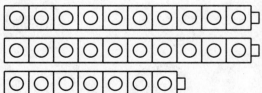

(A) 40 (B) 37 (C) 47 (D) 50

Collecting Coins

NOTE Students practice using coin equivalencies and counting money.

SMH 19, 20

1. Circle coins to show **15¢** in all.

2. Circle coins to show **20¢** in all.

3. Circle coins to show **25¢** in all.

Today's Number: 10

Today's Number is 10.

5 + 5
5 + 3 + 2
11 − 1

Show different ways to make Today's Number.

Tens Go Fish

Imagine you are playing *Tens Go Fish*.
What card would you ask for?

> **NOTE** Students are given one number and must determine what number they need to add to make a total of 10.
>
> **SMH** 46

1.

2.

3.

4.

5.

6.

The Total Is 20

Color the cards in each row that make 20.

NOTE Students find combinations of numbers that equal 20.

SMH **43, 46**

1. | 10 | 5 | 3 | 10 | 1 |

2. | 5 | 8 | 2 | 7 | 5 |

3. | 2 | 1 | 6 | 4 | 9 |

4. | 3 | 5 | 2 | 7 | 5 |

5. | 2 | 7 | 9 | 8 | 1 |

Ongoing Review

6. Which pair of cards has the largest total?

(A) | 3 | 4 |

(B) | 5 | 5 |

(C) | 8 | 9 |

(D) | 7 | 6 |

How Many Children? (page 1 of 2)

Solve the problem. Show your work.
Write an equation.

1. There were 12 children playing tag on the playground.

Then 10 more children joined the game.

How many children are playing tag now?

How Many Children? (page 2 of 2)

Solve the problem. Show your work.
Write an equation.

2. There were 22 children playing tag on the
playground.

Then 10 more children joined the game.

How many children are playing tag now?

Did Problem 1 help you solve Problem 2?
Explain how.

_____

_____

_____

_____

Today's Number: 12

Today's Number is <u>12</u>.

Circle all of the problems that equal Today's Number.

NOTE Students determine which expressions are equal to Today's Number.

 SMH 55

15 − 2	14 − 2
10 + 2 + 0	20 − 6
7 + 7	3 + 2 + 7
10 + 1 + 1	8 + 5
4 + 8	6 + 6

Today's Number: 15

Today's Number is <u>15</u>.

10 + 5
10 + 4 + 1
20 − 5

Show different ways to make Today's Number.

How Many Flowers?

Solve the problem. Show your work.
Write an equation.

Kira picked 12 flowers.
Franco gave her 8 more.
How many flowers does she have now?

> **NOTE** Students solve a story problem about combining two quantities.
>
> **SMH** 59, 60

Today's Number: 13

Today's Number is <u>13</u>.

6 + 7

6 + 4 + 3

15 − 2

Show different ways to make Today's Number.

NOTE Students find combinations of numbers that equal 13. There are many possible solutions.

 55

How Many Cards? (page 1 of 2)

Solve the problem. Show your work.
Write an equation.

1. Kira had 16 baseball cards. She gave 7 of them away. How many baseball cards did Kira have left?

Trading Card

How Many Cards? (page 2 of 2)

Solve the problem. Show your work.
Write an equation.

2. Kira had 26 baseball cards. She gave 7 of them away. How many baseball cards did Kira have left?

Trading Card

Did Problem 1 help you solve Problem 2?
Explain how.

_____

_____

_____

_____

_____

More Than Two to Make Ten

You need three cards to make 10.
What card would you ask for?

NOTE Students are given two numbers and must determine what number they need to add to make a total of 10.

SMH 46

1.

8    1

2.

6    2

3.

2    2

4.

4    3

5.

1    4

6.

7    3

Story Problems (page 1 of 2)

Solve each problem. Show your work.
Write an equation.

1. Franco and Sally have 18 cherries and
   13 grapes.

   How many pieces of fruit do they have?

2. The teacher had 23 new pencils.
   She gave out 12 pencils.
   How many pencils does she have left?

Story Problems (page 2 of 2)

Solve each problem. Show your work.
Write an equation.

3. Sally has 15 pennies.

Jake has 16 pennies.

How many pennies do they have in all?

4. Our class had 22 animal books in
our library.

We loaned 7 of them to another class.

How many animal books do we still have?

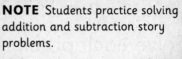

Apple Picking and Apple Pie

Solve each problem. Show your work.
Write an equation.

NOTE Students practice solving addition and subtraction story problems.

SMH 59–61, 67–69

1. Jake and Sally went apple picking.
   Jake picked 8 apples.
   Sally picked 15 apples.
   How many apples did Jake and Sally pick?

2. Kira and Franco had 25 apples.
   They used 6 of the apples to make an apple pie.
   How many apples do they have now?

More Story Problems (page 1 of 2)

Solve each problem. Show your work.
Write an equation.

1. Franco had 30 pennies.

He spent 19 pennies to buy a pencil.

How much money does Franco have left?

2. Kira and Jake made some snowballs.

They each made 16 snowballs.

How many snowballs did they make in all?

More Story Problems (page 2 of 2)

Solve each problem. Show your work.
Write an equation.

3. Jake and Sally were collecting rocks.
Jake found 16 rocks and Sally found 24 rocks.
How many rocks did they collect?

4. There were 32 students in the gym.
15 students went back to their classrooms.
How many students were left in the gym?

Soccer Balls

Solve each problem. Show your work.
Write an equation.

NOTE Students practice solving addition and subtraction story problems.

SMH 59–61, 67–69

1. Sally's soccer team had 27 soccer balls.
   They loaned 9 of them to Franco's team.
   How many soccer balls does Sally's team
   have now?

2. Jake's soccer team had 13 soccer balls.
   Kira's team gave them 11 more balls.
   How many soccer balls does Jake's team
   have now?

How Many Ducks?

Solve the problem. Show your work.
Write an equation.

NOTE Students solve a story problem about combining two quantities.

SMH 59, 60, 61

Yesterday, Sally went to the park.

She saw 19 ducks in the air and 14 ducks in the pond.

How many ducks did she see?

The Doubles Pot

Write the number that comes out—or the
number that is put in.

NOTE Students practice
the doubles combinations.

SMH 47

1.

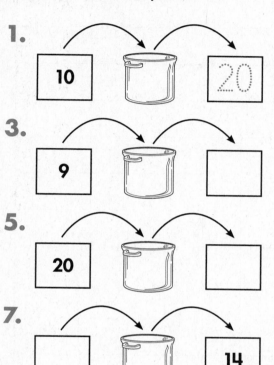

| 10 | | 20 |

2.

| 7 | | |

3.

| 9 | | |

4.

| | | 30 |

5.

| 20 | | |

6.

| 25 | | |

7.

| | | 14 |

8.

| | | 16 |

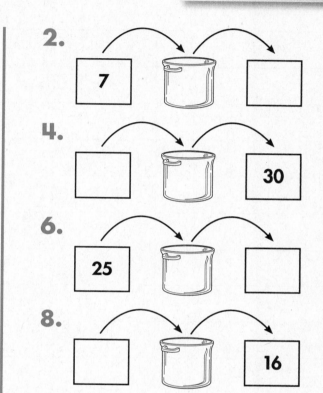

Now, you write two. Make them hard!

9.

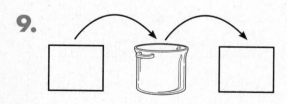

10.

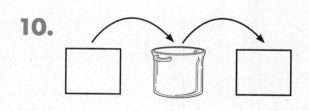

Ongoing Review

11. How many triangles are in this pattern?

(A) 8   (B) 12   (C) 14   (D) 16

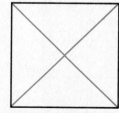

Writing a Magic Pot Problem (page 1 of 2)

NOTE Students write and solve a story problem in which the original number in the problem is doubled.

SMH 47

Tell someone at home the story about the magic pot. Write a Magic Pot problem together on the front of this page. Record your solution to the problem on the back of this page.

Writing a Magic
Pot Problem (page 2 of 2)

Record the solution to your problem here.

Double It Recording Sheet

Pick a card. Double the number. Write the total.

								20
								19
								18
								17
								16
								15
								14
								13
								12
								11
								10
								9
								8
								7
								6
								5
								4
								3
								2

Doubles Arrays Recording Sheet

Pick a card. Double the number. Color that many squares. Write an equation.

3 + 3 = 6

Today's Number: 18

Today's Number is <u>18</u>.

10 + 8

10 + 4 + 4

20 − 2

Show different ways to make Today's Number.

How Many Apples?

Solve the problem. Show your work.
Write an equation.

There were 15 apples in a bowl.
Jake and Sally used 6 of the apples
to make a pie.
How many apples were left?

NOTE Students solve a story problem about subtracting one quantity from another.

SMH **67, 68, 69**

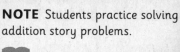

Fish and Sharks

Solve each problem. Show your work.
Write an equation.

NOTE Students practice solving
addition story problems.

SMH 59, 60, 61

1. Franco and Kira went to the aquarium.
Franco counted 16 blue fish.
Kira counted 14 yellow fish.
How many fish did they count altogether?

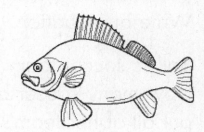

2. In the shark tank, Kira counted 13 sharks
and Franco counted 13 sharks.
How many sharks did they count in all?

Solving a Magic Pot Problem

NOTE Students solve a problem that involves putting something into a magic pot that doubles everything.

SMH 47

Solve the problem. Show your work.
Write an equation.

Sally's soccer team has 17 soccer balls.
How many soccer balls would they have if Sally
put all of her team's balls into the magic pot?

At the Fruit Store

The store where Carla shops sells apples in bags of 5, bananas in bags of 3, and oranges in bags of 4.

1. On Tuesday, Carla bought two bags of fruit.
She got 10 pieces of fruit in all.
What did Carla buy?

2. On Friday, Carla bought 12 pieces of fruit.
What could she have bought?

What else could she have bought?

3. Carla wanted to buy fruit for her 17 friends.
What could she buy?

Complicated Kris Northern

"This image illustrates some of the best qualities of fractals—infinity, reiteration, and self similarity."— **Kris Northern**

Investigations
IN NUMBER, DATA, AND SPACE®

Shapes, Blocks, and Symmetry

Investigation 3

Practicing with Subtraction Cards

NOTE Students practice subtraction facts and use related addition facts to help.

Choose 6 Subtraction Card problems from your "working on" pile, and write these on the blank cards below. Practice these at home with a friend or family member.

____ − ____ = ____ Addition Clue: _____	____ − ____ = ____ Addition Clue: _____
____ − ____ = ____ Addition Clue: _____	____ − ____ = ____ Addition Clue: _____
____ − ____ = ____ Addition Clue: _____	____ − ____ = ____ Addition Clue: _____

Subtraction Facts

Solve the subtraction problems.

NOTE Students solve subtraction problems related to addition combinations.

$10 - 3 =$ ___	$8 - 2 =$ ___	$7 - 5 =$ ___
$9 - 1 =$ ___	$10 - 7 =$ ___	$10 - 4 =$ ___
$8 - 6 =$ ___	$5 - 1 =$ ___	$8 - 7 =$ ___

Write subtraction facts that relate to these addition combinations.

$8 + 1 = 9$	$7 + 2 = 9$	$9 + 1 = 10$
___ $-$ ___ $=$ ___	___ $-$ ___ $=$ ___	___ $-$ ___ $=$ ___
___ $-$ ___ $=$ ___	___ $-$ ___ $=$ ___	___ $-$ ___ $=$ ___

Counting Coins

How many pennies are these coins worth?

NOTE Students practice determining coin equivalencies.

SMH 19, 20

1.

_____ pennies

2.

_____ pennies

3.

_____ pennies

4.

_____ pennies

The Shape of a Face

Find three-dimensional (3-D) objects in your home that have these shapes as one of their faces. For the last object, draw in your own shape.

NOTE Students have been identifying the 2-D faces of 3-D shapes. Students find 3-D shapes at home that have certain 2-D faces.

SMH **113, 122**

Face	3-D Object
□	
▭	
○	
◁	

The Match Game

Match the 3-D block to the 2-D face.

NOTE Students practice identifying the 2-D faces of 3-D shapes.

SMH 122

1.

2.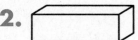

3.

4.

Ongoing Review

5. How many sides does a cube have?

(A) 4   (B) 5   (C) 6   (D) 8

Collecting Leaves

Kira and Franco were collecting leaves.

Kira collected 12 leaves, and Franco collected 13 leaves.

How many leaves did they collect in all?

Solve the problem. Show your work.
Write an equation.

NOTE Students solve a story problem about combining two quantities.

SMH 59, 60, 61

Sail Away!

Tell how many of each kind of block are in the sailboat design. Then follow the directions for coloring.

NOTE Students practice identifying 2-D shapes.

SMH 114

  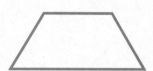 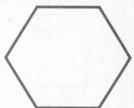

triangle   **rhombus**   **trapezoid**   **hexagon**

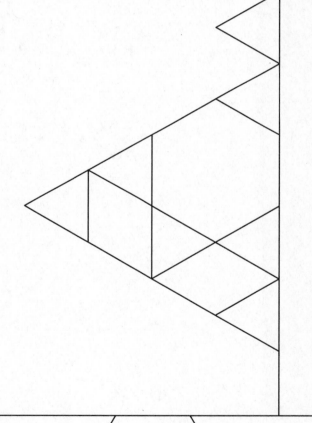

1. Triangles _____
   Color triangles green.

2. Rhombuses _____
   Color rhombuses blue.

3. Trapezoids _____
   Color trapezoids red.

4. Hexagons _____
   Color hexagons yellow.

Build the Geoblock (page 1 of 3)

1. Put Geoblocks together to build this block.
Record your work.

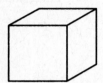

Build the Geoblock (page 2 of 3)

2. Put Geoblocks together to build this block.
Record your work.

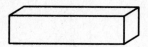

Build the Geoblock (page 3 of 3)

3. Put Geoblocks together to build this block. Record your work.

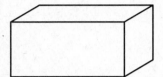

Ways to Fill: Pattern 2 (page 1 of 2)

Use different types of pattern blocks to fill the
shape. Record your work by tracing the shapes
of the blocks you used onto each shape outline.

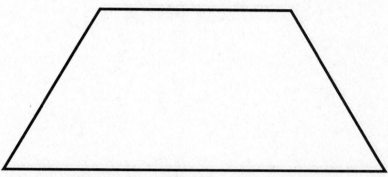

Use 1 type of pattern block to fill the shape.

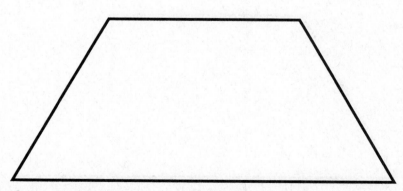

Use 2 types of pattern blocks to fill the shape.

Ways to Fill: Pattern 2 (page 2 of 2)

Use different types of pattern blocks to fill the
shape. Record your work by tracing the shapes
of the blocks you used onto each shape outline.

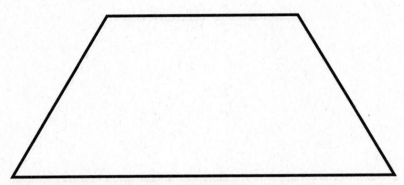

Use 3 types of pattern blocks to fill the shape.

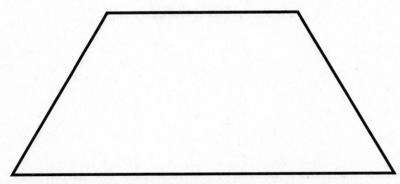

Use 4 types of pattern blocks to fill the shape.

Rhombus Cover Up

Look at the rhombus at the right. Draw lines to show how you could use it to cover each figure. Then tell how many rhombuses are in each figure.

> **NOTE** Students determine how many rhombuses are needed to cover each shape.
>
> SMH 114

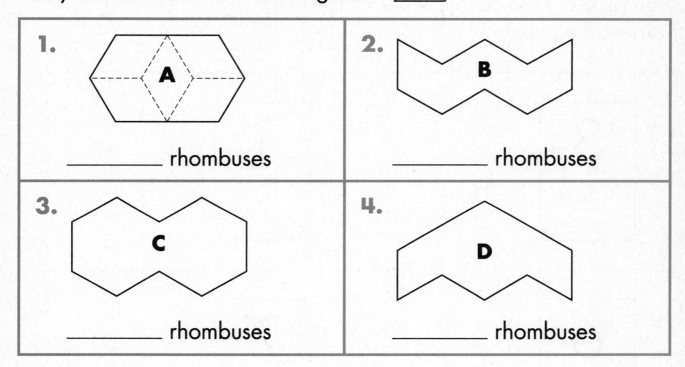

1.

A

_____ rhombuses

2.

B

_____ rhombuses

3.

C

_____ rhombuses

4.

D

_____ rhombuses

5. Which figure has the **most** rhombuses? Figure _____

6. Which figure has the **fewest** rhombuses? Figure _____

Ongoing Review

7. What numbers are missing?

1, 2, 3 ____, 5, 6, 7, ____

4 and 5   4 and 8   7 and 8   3 and 4

Ⓐ   Ⓑ   Ⓒ   Ⓓ

Doubles Combinations Practice

Imagine that you are playing Double It. Below are the cards you picked. Find each double. Write an equation.

Example:

8

$8 + 8 = 16$

NOTE Students practice the doubles combinations.

SMH 47

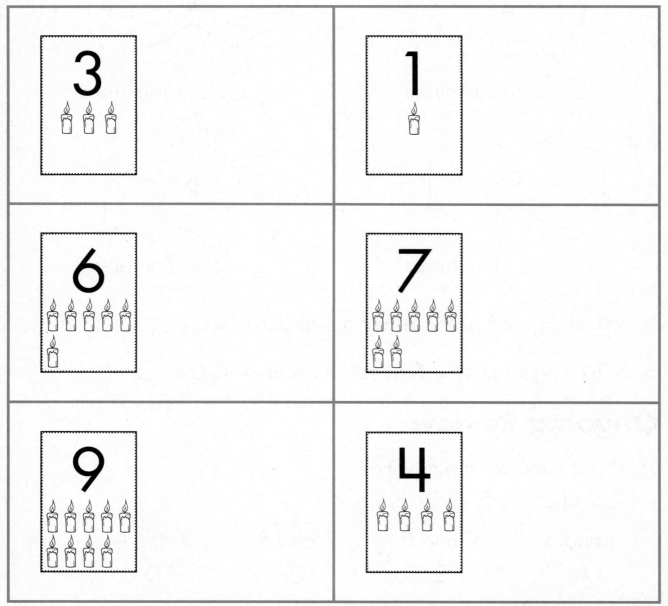

3

1

6

7

9

4

© Pearson Education 2

Shapes at Home

Draw pictures of at least 5 shapes that you find at home. Write the name of each object and what shape it is.

NOTE Students have been identifying and working with different types of 2-D and 3-D shapes. Students identify shapes at home, draw them, and record their names.

SMH 114, 117, 122

Example: A door is shaped like a rectangle.	

More Than Two to Make Ten

NOTE Students are given two numbers and determine the number they need to add to make a total of 10.

SMH 46

Pretend you are playing the card game *More Than 2 to Make 10*. What card would you need to make 10?

7	1	
3	2	
1	1	

2	2	
5	2	
1	9	

Identifying Different Types of Quadrilaterals

Color the shapes that have 4 sides and 4 right angles **blue**. Color the shapes that have 4 sides, but not 4 right angles **red**.

NOTE Students sort shapes into 2 categories: "4 Sides and 4 Right Angles" and "4 Sides, but not Right Angles." Students identify these groups of shapes and color them either blue or red.

SMH **118, 119, 120**

Which One Has the Most?

Look at the rectangles on Which Is Biggest? Record how many tiles you need to cover each rectangle.

Rectangle	A	B	C	D	E	F	G
Number of Tiles to Cover							

Imagine that the rectangles are chocolate bars.

1. Which chocolate bar would you want? _____
   Why?

   _____

   _____

2. Which chocolate bar would have the most chocolate? _____
   How do you know?

   _____

   _____

3. Which chocolate bar would have the least chocolate? _____
   How do you know?

   _____

   _____

Which Is Biggest?
Which Is Smallest?

NOTE Students count the number of square units to order a set of rectangles by their area.

SMH 127

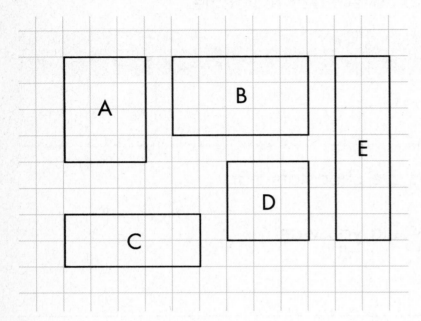

1. Count the squares in each rectangle.

_____ _____ _____ _____ _____
   A   B   C   D   E

2. Which rectangle is biggest? _____

3. Which rectangle is smallest? _____

4. Write the letters of the rectangles in order from biggest to smallest.

_____ _____ _____ _____ _____

Rectangle Riddles (page 1 of 2)

Use color tiles to solve each riddle. Draw a picture of your solution.

1. This rectangle has 5 rows. It has 25 tiles.

2. This rectangle has 3 rows. There are 7 tiles in each row.

3. This rectangle has 11 tiles.

Rectangle Riddles (page 2 of 2)

Use color tiles to solve each riddle. Draw a picture
of your solution.

4. This rectangle has 3 columns and 3 rows.

5. This rectangle has 15 tiles. It has 3 columns.

6. Write a rectangle riddle of your own.

_____

_____

_____

_____

Double It Recording Sheet

Pick a card. Double the number. Write the total.

								20
								19 20
								18
								17
								16
								15
								14
								13
								12
								11
								10
								9
								8
								7
								6
								5
								4
								3
								2

Stickers for the Class

There are 23 students in Mr. Z's class.
Mr. Z has 19 stickers.

Mr. Z wants to give 1 sticker to
each student.

1. Are there enough for the class?   YES   NO

2. Are there any extra stickers?   YES   NO

    How many? _____

3. Does Mr. Z need more stickers?   YES   NO

    How many? _____

4. How did you figure it out? Show your work.

The Rectangle Riddler

Draw the rectangle that solves the riddle.

NOTE Students practice drawing rectangles based on given information about dimensions and area.

 126, 127

1. I have 4 rows and 6 columns.

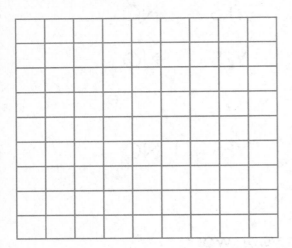

2. I have 15 squares and 3 rows.

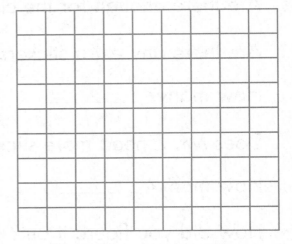

3. I have 6 rows and 5 columns.

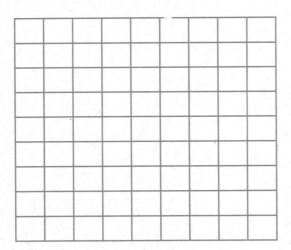

4. I have 18 squares and 6 columns.

5. In the problems above, which rectangle is the largest? _____

Numbers in Sequence

1. Solve these problems. Fill in the totals on the 100 chart below.

NOTE Students practice the "Plus 1, Plus 2," "Doubles Combinations," and sequencing numbers 1–100.

SMH 24, 25

$9 + 9 =$ _____ $0 + 1 =$ _____ $1 + 6 =$ _____

$9 + 2 =$ _____ $9 + 1 =$ _____ $3 + 1 =$ _____

$10 + 10 =$ _____ $3 + 3 =$ _____ $8 + 8 =$ _____

$7 + 7 =$ _____ $2 + 7 =$ _____ $6 + 6 =$ _____

2. Fill in the other missing numbers on the 100 chart.

	2	3		5			8		
				15		17		19	
21	22	23	24		26	27		29	30
			34	35	36	37	38		40
41	42		44		46		48	49	
	52	53	54	55	56				60
61	62	63		65		67	68	69	70
71			74	75	76	77	78	79	80
	82		84	85	86	87	88	89	90
91	92	93	94	95	96	97		99	

Only One Rectangle
(page 1 of 3)

Cut the tiles on Only One Rectangle (M27). Use the tiles to make rectangles. For each box, draw all of the rectangles you make with that number of tiles. Make rectangles using 2 tiles up to 7 tiles. If you want to, make rectangles using 8 tiles through 12 tiles. Be sure to answer the question on the last page.

> **NOTE** Today in class students used square tiles to make different sized rectangles. They found that for certain numbers of tiles, they could make only one rectangle. Tonight, students will work on a similar activity and determine for which quantities of tiles only one rectangle is possible.
>
> **SMH** 127

Use **2** tiles.	Use **3** tiles.
Use **4** tiles.	Use **5** tiles.

Only One Rectangle (page 2 of 3)

Use the tiles you already cut to make rectangles. For each box, draw all of the rectangles you make with that number of tiles.

Use **6** tiles.	Use **7** tiles.
Use **8** tiles.	Use **9** tiles.

Only One Rectangle (page 3 of 3)

Use the tiles you already cut to make rectangles. For each box, draw all of the rectangles you make with that number of tiles.

Use **10** tiles.
Use **11** tiles.
Use **12** tiles.

Which numbers of tiles make only 1 rectangle? _____

© Pearson Education 2

Double Trouble

Look at each problem. If the answer is wrong, cross it out and write the correct answer.

NOTE Students practice the doubles combinations.

SMH 47

For example:

$2 + 2 = \cancel{3}$ 4

1. $4 + 4 = 10$	**2.** $5 + 5 = 10$
3. $6 + 6 = 11$	**4.** $9 + 9 = 16$
5. $7 + 7 = 15$	**6.** $3 + 3 = 5$
7. $8 + 8 = 14$	**8.** $10 + 10 = 20$

Ongoing Review

9. Which answer could **not** be correct?

Shannon has 12 pets. Some of them are cats, and some of them are dogs. How many of Shannon's 12 pets might be cats?

(A) 12   (B) 11   (C) 6   (D) 1

Double Arrays

Pick a card. Double the number. Color that many squares. Write an equation.

NOTE Students draw arrays of a doubles fact and then write an equation to match the array.

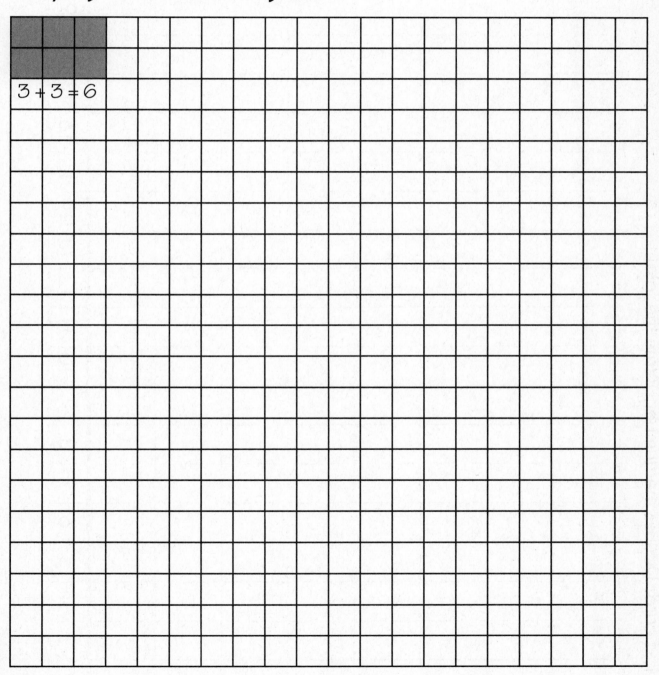

3 + 3 = 6

Double It Recording Sheet

NOTE Students practice adding doubles.

Pick a card. Double the number. Write the total.

								20
								19
								18
								17
								16
								15
								14
								13
								12
								11
								10
								9
								8
								7
								6
								5
								4
								3
								2

Sharing Balloons

Sally had 21 balloons.
She gave 9 of them to Max.
How many balloons does Sally have now?

Solve the problem. Show your work.
Write an equation.

> **NOTE** Students solve a story problem about subtracting one quantity from another.
>
> **SMH** 67, 68, 69

Ongoing Review

1. Which shape has the most sides?

 rhombus   triangle   Ⓒ square   Ⓓ hexagon

Today's Number: 16

Circle all of the problems that equal Today's Number.

NOTE Students identify expressions that equal the number 16.

SMH 55, 56

Today's Number is <u>16</u>.

19 − 2	8 + 8
5 + 5 + 6	20 − 4
4 + 4 + 4 + 4	4 + 9
16 + 3	10 + 6
2 + 14	8 + 2 + 3 + 3

Fly Away!

Tell how many of each kind of block are in the kite design. Then follow the directions for coloring.

NOTE Students practice identifying 2-D shapes.

SMH 114

triangle   pentagon   trapezoid   hexagon

1. Triangles _____
Color triangles green.

2. Pentagons _____
Color pentagons blue.

3. Trapezoids _____
Color trapezoids red.

4. Hexagons _____
Color hexagons yellow.

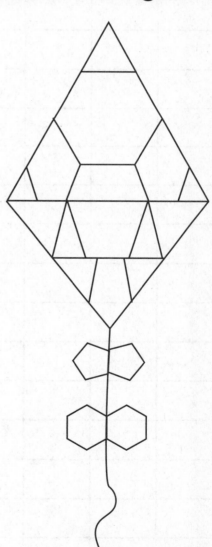

Double It Recording Sheet

Pick a card. Double the number. Write the total.

								20
								19
								18
								17
								16
								15
								14
								13
								12
								11
								10
								9
								8
								7
								6
								5
								4
								3
								2

Tens Go Fish Practice

Imagine that you are playing the card game *Tens Go Fish*. What card would you ask for?

NOTE Students are given one number and determine which number they need to add to make 10.

SMH 46, G14

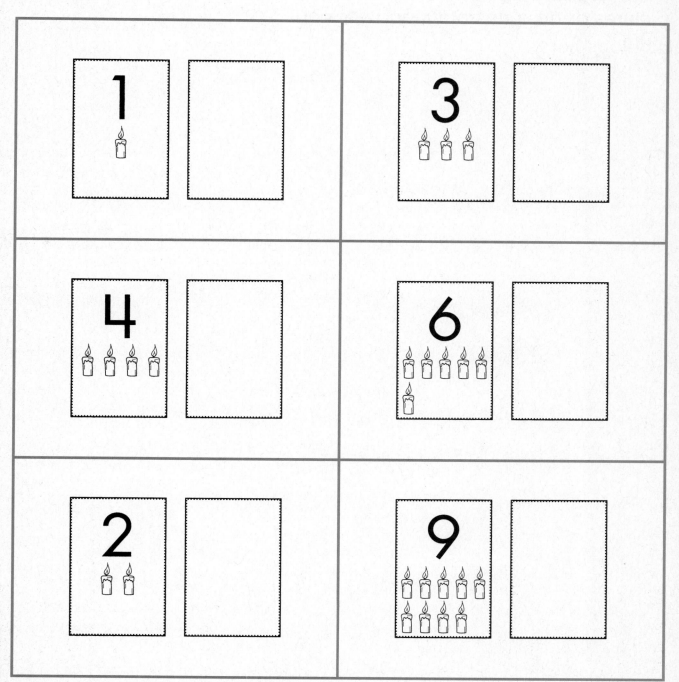

Looking for Symmetry

Look around your home for at least 5 things that are symmetrical. Draw pictures of them or glue symmetrical pictures or designs from magazines or catalogs here.

NOTE Students find symmetrical objects at home.

 129

Copy Tiles Grid Paper

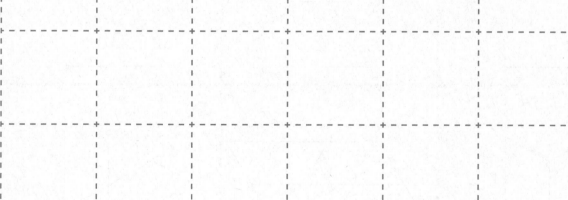

Mirror Symmetry

Tell whether each pattern block design is symmetrical. Write **yes** or **no.**

NOTE Students determine if a shape is symmetrical.

 129

1.

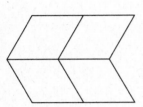

_____

2.

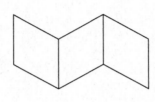

_____

3.

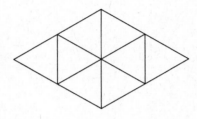

_____

4.

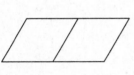

_____

5.

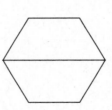

_____

6.

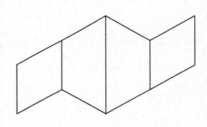

_____

7.

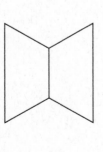

_____

8.

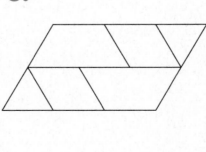

_____

9.

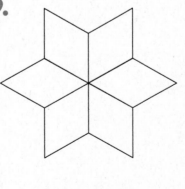

_____

Time by the Hour
Read each clock and write the time.

NOTE Students practice telling time to the hour.

SMH 135

1.

   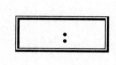

2.

   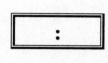

3.

   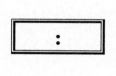

4.

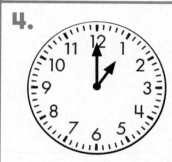   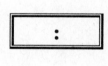

5.

   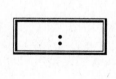

6.

   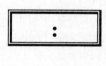

7.

   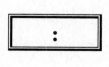

8.

   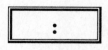

Half and Half (page 1 of 2)

Side B

Side A

Half and Half (page 2 of 2)

Side B

Side A

How Many Blocks? (page 1 of 2)

Use this sheet with the Half and Half sheet and
your pattern blocks.

Pattern Block Design 1

1. Build Side A of your design.

2. Number of blocks in Side A: _____

3. I think there will be _____ blocks in the
whole design because:

_____

_____

_____

_____

4. Build Side B to finish your design.

5. How many blocks are in your finished design? _____

How Many Blocks? (page 2 of 2)

Use this sheet with the Half and Half sheet and
your pattern blocks.

Pattern Block Design 2

1. Build Side A of your design.

2. Number of blocks in Side A: _____

3. I think there will be _____ blocks in the
whole design because:

_____

_____

_____

_____

4. Build Side B to finish your design.

5. How many blocks are in your finished design? _____

Finish the Shapes

Draw the other half of the shape to make it symmetrical.

NOTE Students complete each shape to make it symmetrical.

SMH **129**

1. Example:

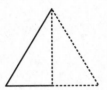

2.

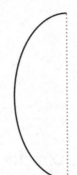

3.

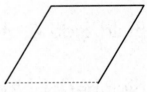

4.

5.

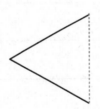

6.

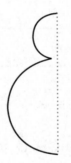

7.

8.

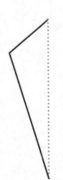

9.

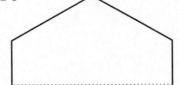

Symmetry in Nature

Many objects in the natural world are symmetrical. Look at the pictures below and draw as many lines of symmetry as possible.

NOTE Students look for lines of symmetry on real-world objects.

SMH 129

"This image illustrates some of the best qualities of fractals—infinity, reiteration, and self similarity."– **Kris Northern**

Investigations
IN NUMBER, DATA, AND SPACE®

Stickers, Number Strings, and Story Problems

Investigation 3

Problems About Three Groups (page 1 of 2)

Find the number of cubes Jake used in each problem. Add the numbers in at least two different orders. Show your work.

1. Jake used 6 green cubes, 3 blue cubes, and 4 yellow cubes to make a train. How many cubes did he use?

2. Jake used 8 green cubes, 5 blue cubes, and 5 yellow cubes to make a train. How many cubes did he use?

Problems About Three Groups (page 2 of 2)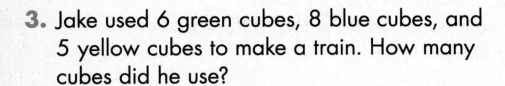

3. Jake used 6 green cubes, 8 blue cubes, and 5 yellow cubes to make a train. How many cubes did he use?

4. When you change the order of the numbers, do you get the same answer? Why do you think so?

Today's Number: 17

Today's Number is *17*.

10 + 7

5 + 5 + 5 + 2

20 − 3

Write at least 5 different ways to make 17.

NOTE Students write equations that equal today's number. There are many possible solutions.

 55, 56

Number Strings (page 1 of 2)

Use combinations you know to solve each problem.

1. $3 + 4 + 6 =$	**2.** $3 + 7 + 8 =$
3. $7 + 5 + 7 + 5 =$	**4.** $1 + 5 + 9 =$
5. $8 + 4 + 2 =$	**6.** $8 + 6 + 3 + 7 + 2 =$

Number Strings (page 2 of 2)

7. $8 + 9 + 3 =$	**8.** $6 + 6 + 7 + 7 =$
9. $8 + 6 + 8 + 4 =$	**10.** $3 + 7 + 4 =$
11. $9 + 4 + 5 + 1 =$	**12.** $8 + 6 + 3 + 7 + 2 =$

Practicing Number Strings

> **NOTE** Students practice solving problems with several addends and using addition combinations they know.
>
> **SMH** 46, 47, 54

Solve each number string problem. Remember to look for doubles and for combinations that make 10.

1. $3 + 4 + 7 =$	**2.** $1 + 2 + 7 + 4 =$
3. $8 + 10 + 8 =$	**4.** $2 + 9 + 8 + 1 =$
5. $6 + 5 + 4 + 5 =$	**6.** $2 + 6 + 6 =$
7. $9 + 3 + 1 + 3 =$	**8.** $5 + 7 + 3 + 5 + 6 =$

Practicing with Subtraction Cards

> **NOTE** Students practice subtraction facts and use related addition facts to help.

Choose 6 Subtraction Card problems from your "working on" pile. Write the subtraction sentences on the blank cards below, and then practice them at home with a friend or family member.

____ – ____ = ____ Addition Clue: _____	____ – ____ = ____ Addition Clue: _____
____ – ____ = ____ Addition Clue: _____	____ – ____ = ____ Addition Clue: _____
____ – ____ = ____ Addition Clue: _____	____ – ____ = ____ Addition Clue: _____

Can You Make . . . ?

Use three different numbers in each problem.
Use each number below at least once.

NOTE Students practice finding combinations of three addends to make a certain sum.

SMH 54

7		8		9		1		4
	5		3		6		2	

1. Can you make 15 with 3 numbers?

_____ + _____ + _____ = 15

2. Can you make 16 with 3 numbers?

_____ + _____ + _____ = 16

3. Can you make 17 with 3 numbers?

_____ + _____ + _____ = 17

4. Can you make 18 with 3 numbers?

_____ + _____ + _____ = 18

Number Strings at Home

Use combinations you know to solve these problems. Show your work.

NOTE Students solve two problems with several addends. Encourage your child to use addition combinations he or she knows, and to record all work.

SMH **43, 54**

1. $6 + 7 + 5 + 6 + 3 =$

2. $8 + 3 + 4 + 6 + 2 =$

Close to 20 Recording Sheet

Score

Game

Round 1: _____ + _____ + _____ = _____

Round 2: _____ + _____ + _____ = _____

Round 3: _____ + _____ + _____ = _____

Round 4: _____ + _____ + _____ = _____

Round 5: _____ + _____ + _____ = _____

TOTAL SCORE _____

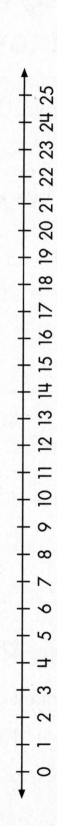

Looking for Combinations

Solve the same number string three different ways. Use equations to show your solution.

NOTE Students practice using combinations they know to solve a problem with several addends.

SMH 43, 46, 47, 48, 54

1. Begin by looking for combinations of 10.

   ✓ ✓

   $6 + 4 + 5 + 7 + 4$

   $6 + 4 = 10$

2. Begin by looking for doubles.

   $6 + 4 + 5 + 7 + 4$

3. Begin by looking for near doubles.

   $6 + 4 + 5 + 7 + 4$

Ongoing Review

4. Which number combination does **not** make 20?

   Ⓐ $10 + 10$

   Ⓑ $18 + 2$

   Ⓒ $19 + 3$

   Ⓓ $5 + 5 + 5 + 5$

More Number Strings (page 1 of 2)

Use combinations you know to solve these problems.
Show your work.

1. $2 + 7 + 6 =$	**2.** $5 + 3 + 6 + 8 + 7 =$
3. $5 + 6 + 4 + 10 + 5 =$	**4.** $2 + 9 + 1 + 2 =$
5. $5 + 6 + 4 =$	**6.** $9 + 7 + 1 + 3 =$

More Number Strings (page 2 of 2)

7. 11 + 11 + 8 =

8. 5 + 4 + 7 + 5 + 7 =

9. 12 + 4 + 4 + 10 =

10. 9 + 8 + 11 + 8 =

11. 19 + 6 + 5 =

12. 9 + 6 + 1 + 4 =

Even More Number Strings (page 1 of 2)

Use combinations you know to solve these problems.
Show your work.

1. 9 + 8 + 7 =	**2.** 2 + 3 + 3 + 3 + 7 =
3. 9 + 7 + 3 + 11 =	**4.** 9 + 8 + 17 =
5. 6 + 6 + 6 =	**6.** 19 + 7 + 3 + 11 =

Even More Number Strings (page 2 of 2)

7. 6 + 6 + 8 =

8. 12 + 18 + 5 =

9. 6 + 7 + 9 + 9 =

10. 6 + 6 + 8 + 10 =

11. 15 + 8 + 5 =

12. 9 + 16 + 1 + 14 =

Time: Half Hours

1. Read each clock and write the time.

NOTE Students practice telling time to the half hour.

SMH 139

2. What is the same about all of these clocks? Why? (Hint: Look at the big hand.)

Scores in *Close to 20*

Sally and Franco are playing *Close to 20*.
Fill in the rest of Franco's sheet.

> **NOTE** Students solve addition problems with three addends and determine how far the totals are from 20.
>
> **SMH** 43, 54

Remember: The score for a round is how far the total for that round is from 20.

Sally's Score Sheet:

		Total	Score
Round 1	4 + 6 + 8	18	2
Round 2	10 + 9 + 3	22	2
Round 3	9 + 0 + 10	19	1
Round 4	10 + 1 + 1	12	8
Round 5	10 + 2 + 8	20	0

Sally's Total Score: _____

Franco's Score Sheet:

		Total	Score
Round 1	4 + 8 + 2		
Round 2	6 + 9 + 5		
Round 3	7 + 6 + 8		
Round 4	3 + 5 + 10		
Round 5	1 + 7 + 9		

Franco's Total Score: _____

Close to 20 Recording Sheet

NOTE Students have been playing "Close to 20" in class. As you play together, ask your child to help you find combinations close to 20.

SMH 43, 44, 45, 46, 47, 48–50, 52, 53, 54

Score

Game

Round 1: _____ + _____ + _____ = _____

Round 2: _____ + _____ + _____ = _____

Round 3: _____ + _____ + _____ = _____

Round 4: _____ + _____ + _____ = _____

Round 5: _____ + _____ + _____ = _____

TOTAL SCORE _____

How Many Rocks?

Solve each problem. Show your work.
Write an equation.

1. Kira and Jake collected rocks. Kira
found 12 rocks and Jake found
24 rocks. How many rocks did
they collect?

2. Kira collected 26 rocks. Jake
collected 14 rocks. How many
rocks did they collect?

How Many Shells?

Solve each problem. Show your work.
Write an equation.

1. Sally and Franco went to the beach. Sally found 23 shells and Franco found 14 shells. How many shells did they find?

2. Yesterday, Sally and Franco collected 27 shells. Today, they collected 13 more shells. How many shells did they collect?

How Many Cars?

Solve each problem. Show your work.
Write an equation.

NOTE Students solve story problems about adding two quantities.

SMH **59, 60, 61**

1. Sally and Franco were taking a trip with their parents. While they were driving, Sally counted 21 blue cars. Franco counted 17 blue cars. How many blue cars did they count?

2. On the trip home, Sally counted 16 trucks. Franco counted 13 trucks. How many trucks did they count?

Ongoing Review

3. How many students were absent on March 3?

   (A) 3   (C) 1

   (B) 2   (D) 0

Date	Present	Absent	Total
March 1	26	2	28
March 2	28	0	28
March 3	25	?	28

How Many Cherries?

Solve each problem. Show your work.
Write an equation.

NOTE Students combine two
quantities to solve a story problem.
Encourage your child to use
combinations he or she knows,
and to record all work.

SMH 59, 60, 61

1. Sally picked 15 cherries. Jake picked
   16 cherries. How many cherries did
   they pick?

2. After picking so many cherries, Sally and Jake
   were hungry. Sally ate 11 cherries, and Jake ate
   17 cherries. How many cherries did they eat?

How Many Marbles?

Solve each problem. Show your work.
Write an equation.

1. Kira had 35 marbles in her bag. She gave 12 of them to Franco. How many marbles did she have left in her bag?

2. Jake had 45 marbles. He gave 22 of them to his little brother. How many marbles does Jake have left?

Today's Number: 19

Today's Number is 19. Circle all the problems that equal Today's Number.

NOTE Students determine which expressions are equal to 19.

 55

$5 + 5 + 5 + 4$	$21 - 6$
$10 + 9 + 0$	$23 - 4$
$6 + 7 + 8$	$2 + 3 + 3 + 4 + 7$
$3 + 8 + 2 + 3 + 3$	$9 + 9 + 1$
$27 - 9$	$7 + 7 + 2 + 2 + 1$

How Many Pennies? (page 1 of 2)

Solve each problem. Show your work.
Write an equation.

1. Sally saved 13 pennies. Then her mom gave her 12 more pennies. How many pennies does she have now?

2. Franco had 25 pennies. Then he gave 13 pennies to his little brother. How many pennies does Franco have left?

How Many Pennies? (page 2 of 2)

3. Kira had 27 pennies. Then her mom gave her 12 more pennies. How many pennies does she have now?

4. Franco had 39 pennies. Then he gave 12 pennies to his little brother. How many pennies does Franco have left?

How Many Children?

Solve each problem. Show your work.
Write an equation.

NOTE Students solve story problems that involve subtracting one quantity from another.

SMH **67, 68, 69**

1. There were 28 children in the pool. At lunchtime, 11 children got out of the pool. How many children were still in the pool?

2. Ms. Walter has 20 children in her class. On Monday, 9 children were absent. How many children were in class?

Ongoing Review

3. Which number is 10 **more** than 21 and 10 **less** than 41?

(A) 40   (B) 31   (C) 30   (D) 22

How Many Books?

Solve each problem. Show your work.
Write an equation.

NOTE Students solve a story problem that involves subtracting one quantity from another. Encourage your child to record all work.

SMH 67, 68

1. Our class has 29 reptile books. We lent 7 of them to another class. How many reptile books do we still have?

2. Our class also has 24 bird books. We lent 9 of them to another class. How many bird books do we still have?

Balloons and Children (page 1 of 2)

Solve each problem. Show your work.
Write an equation.

1. Kira had a bunch of 18 balloons. Sally gave her some more balloons. Kira then had 24 balloons. How many balloons did Sally give to Kira?

2. Franco had 24 balloons. He let go of some by mistake, and they flew away. When he counted again, he had 18 balloons left. How many balloons flew away?

3. Can you use what you know from Problem 1 to help you solve Problem 2? How does it help?

Balloons and Children (page 2 of 2)

4. There were 23 children on the playground. Some of those children left. Now there are 14 children on the playground. How many children left?

5. There were 14 children on the playground. Some more children came to join them. Now there are 23 children on the playground. How many children came?

6. Can you use what you know from Problem 4 to help you solve Problem 5? How does it help?

Roll and Double

You are playing a game called *Roll and Double*. These dot cubes show your rolls. Find the total of each roll. Then find the double of that total. Write an equation.

> **NOTE** Students practice adding two numbers and solving doubles combinations.
>
> **SMH** 43, 47

1.	**2.**
3.	**4.**
5.	**6.**

Birds, Fish, and Marbles (page 1 of 2)

Solve each problem. Show your work. Write an equation.

1. Jake had some marbles in a bag. He won 20 more marbles in a game. Now Jake has 29 marbles in his bag. How many marbles did Jake start with?

2. There were some birds sitting on a wire. 15 more birds joined them. Now there are 35 birds on the wire. How many birds were on the wire to begin with?

Birds, Fish, and Marbles (page 2 of 2)

3. Kira has a collection of marbles. She gave 12 marbles to Jake. Now Kira has 20 marbles left in her collection. How many marbles did Kira start with?

4. The pet store has a tank of goldfish. On Friday the store sold 10 goldfish. There are 20 goldfish left in the tank. How many goldfish were in the tank to begin with?

Solve the Equation

Solve each equation.

____ + 6 = 10	____ + 8 = 16	____ + 7 = 9
____ + 10 = 20	____ + 5 = 10	____ + 10 = 14
____ − 6 = 6	____ − 5 = 1	14 − ____ = 7
10 − ____ = 3	____ − 10 = 8	18 − ____ = 9

Cover Up Recording Sheet

Choose a total number. Count out that many
objects. Player 1 hides some of the objects.
Player 2 figures out how many are hidden.

Total Number	Number Not Covered	Number Covered
_____	_____	_____
_____	_____	_____
_____	_____	_____
_____	_____	_____
_____	_____	_____
_____	_____	_____
_____	_____	_____
_____	_____	_____
_____	_____	_____

How Many Points?
How Many Cards?

Solve each problem. Show your work.
Write an equation.

> **NOTE** Students practice solving problems where one part of the problem is unknown.
>
> **SMH** 76–80

1. In the first half of a basketball game, the Wizards scored 15 points. At the end of the game they had 26 points. How many points did the Wizards score in the second half?

2. Sally had 28 basketball cards. She gave some of the cards to her brother. Now she has 18 basketball cards. How many cards did Sally give to her brother?

Ongoing Review

3. Which number string is **less** than 20?

(A) $8 + 6 + 4 + 4$

(C) $8 + 4 + 2 + 5$

(B) $9 + 3 + 7 + 5$

(D) $6 + 5 + 9 + 1$

Tell a Story

Write a story problem for each equation.
Solve the problems.

NOTE Writing their own story problem for a given expression helps students learn to connect the numbers and symbols to the actions they represent.

SMH 59, 61, 67, 69

1. $8 + 9 =$

2. $14 - 4 =$

Story Problems (page 1 of 2)

Solve each problem. Show your work.
Write an equation.

1. Kira had 30 pennies in her piggy bank. She spent
   19 pennies at the store. How many pennies does
   Kira have left?

2. Sally and Jake were making snowballs. They
   each made 18 snowballs. How many snowballs
   did they make in all?

Story Problems (page 2 of 2)

3. Jake had 12 marbles. Kira gave him some more. Now he has 23 marbles. How many marbles did Kira give to Jake?

4. Our class had 22 animal books. We lent 9 of them to another class. How many animal books do we still have?

More Story Problems (page 1 of 2)

Solve each problem. Show your work.
Write an equation.

1. Our class went on a trip to the zoo. There were 23 students and 9 adults on the trip. How many people went on the zoo trip?

2. Sally saw 27 ducks in the pond. Some of the ducks flew away. When she counted again, there were 16 ducks in the pond. How many ducks flew away?

More Story Problems (page 2 of 2)

3. Sally had 35 pennies. Some of the pennies fell out of her pocket. When Sally got to the store, she had 22 pennies. How many pennies fell out of her pocket?

4. There were 13 children playing in the park. Some more children came to play. Then there were 36 children at the park. How many children came to play?

How Many Apples?

Solve the problem. Show your work.
Write an equation.

NOTE Students solve a story problem that involves subtracting one quantity from another.

SMH **67, 68, 69**

1. Franco picked 27 apples. He used 18 of them to make an apple pie. How many apples does he have left?

Ongoing Review

2. Which subtraction expression is **more** than 20?

(A) 30 − 18

(B) 30 − 14

(C) 30 − 11

(D) 30 − 8

A Problem About *Cover Up*

NOTE Students solve a story problem where one part of the problem is unknown. Encourage your child to record all work.

Solve the problem. Show your work.

Kira and Franco were playing *Cover Up* with buttons. They had 24 buttons. Franco hid some of them. When Kira opened her eyes, she counted 17 buttons. How many buttons did Franco hide?

Write a Story Problem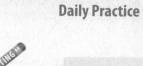

Write a story problem for each expression.
Solve the problems.

1. 16 + 22 = _____

NOTE Writing their own story problem for a given expression helps students learn to connect the numbers and symbols to the actions they represent.

SMH 59, 60, 61, 67, 68, 69

2. 20 − 17 = _____

Ongoing Review

3. Which equation does **not** equal 10?

(A) 10 − 10 = _____

(B) 15 − 5 = _____

(C) 19 − 9 = _____

(D) 20 − 10 = _____

Partners and Teams

Fill in the table.

How many would not have a partner?	Would everyone have a partner? If yes, how many pairs?	Number of students	Would there be two equal teams? If yes, how many on each team?	How many would be left over?
		7		
		9		
		10		
		11		
		12		
		16		
		20		

More Partners and Teams

Fill in the table.

How many would be left over?	Would there be two equal teams? If yes, how many on each team?	Number of students	Would everyone have a partner? If yes, how many pairs?	How many would not have a partner?

How Many Flowers?

Solve the problem. Show your work.
Write an equation.

Kira picked 15 flowers. Franco gave her some more. Now Kira has 23 flowers. How many flowers did Franco give to Kira?

NOTE Students solve an addition problem where one part is missing.

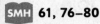 **61, 76–80**

Problems About Partners and Teams

Solve each problem. Show your work.

NOTE Students are thinking about numbers that can and cannot make groups of two, or two equal teams, as they investigate odd and even numbers.

 41–42

1. 13 children are taking an art class. If they pair off, will everyone have a partner?

2. There are 14 children on the playground. Can they make two equal teams to play kickball?

Questions About Even and Odd Numbers (page 1 of 2)

Choose one question to investigate. Use cubes, drawings, numbers, or other math tools to show your thinking.

1. On our "Partners and Teams" chart, every number has only 0 or 1 left over. Could there ever be 3 or 4 left over? Why do you think so?

Would **any** number have only 0 or 1 left over? Why do you think so?

Questions About Even and Odd Numbers (page 2 of 2) ✏️ WRITING

2. On our "Partners and Teams" chart, every number that makes 2 equal teams **also** makes partners. Why do you think so?

Would this be true for **any** number? Explain your thinking.

How Many Pockets?

NOTE Students practice addition combinations by solving a problem with several addends.

SMH 43, 46, 54

1. How many pockets are these students wearing today? Find combinations of 10 to help you add.

Students	Number of Pockets
Howard	4
Hope	2
Mike	3
Tony	5
Tamara	0
Mark	1
Holly	4
Sarah	4
Timothy	7
Maria	5
Vipan	1
Titus	1
Scott	0
Hadiya	2
Harry	6
Rick	4
Michelle	4
Martha	7
Sean	2
Thomas	3

10

GRAND TOTAL

_____

Ongoing Review

2. Which number combination does **not** make 50?

(A) 25 + 25

(B) 35 + 15

(C) 41 + 10

(D) 42 + 8

30: Odd or Even?

Read the problem. Explain your thinking.

Sally thinks that 30 is odd because
3 is odd. Do you agree with her?
Why or why not?

> **NOTE** Students explain how they know a number is even or odd. They may use words, numbers, and drawings to explain their thinking.
>
> **SMH** 41–42

Draw a picture or diagram to help Sally
understand your thinking.

How Many Legs?

Solve the problem. Show how you figured it out.

How many legs are in your class? _____

How Many Student Legs?

NOTE Students practice counting by groups of 2.

SMH 37

1. Count by 2s. Record your counting.

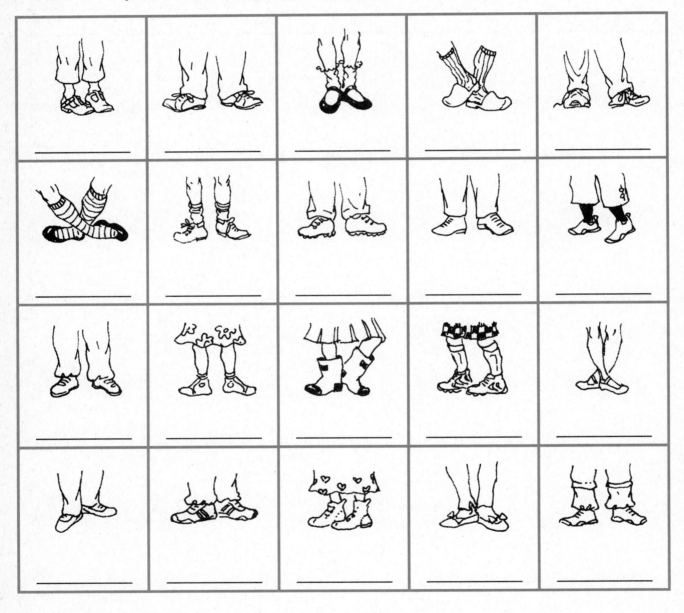

2. The legs above belong to the students in Room 110. How many students are there in Room 110? How many legs?

How Many Fingers?

Solve the problem. Show how you figured it out.

How many fingers are in your class? _____

How Many Toes?
How Many People?

NOTE Students practice counting by groups of 10.

SMH 39

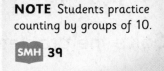

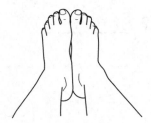

1. If there are 10 toes, how many people are there? _____

2. If there are 50 toes, how many people are there? _____

3. If there are 100 toes, how many people are there? _____

4. If there are 150 toes, how many people are there? _____

5. If there are 200 toes, how many people are there? _____

6. What pattern do you see?

Ongoing Review

7. What comes next?

 ____, ____, ____,

Ways to Make 20¢

NOTE Students practice finding possible combinations of coins to equal a given amount.

SMH 19, 20

1. Find all the ways to make 20¢.

Pennies	Nickels	Dimes
20	0	0

HINT: If you have a different set of coins for each row, then you have found all the possible ways.

2. What is the fewest number of coins that make 20¢? _____

Ongoing Review

3. You have 14¢. You need 20¢. How much **more** do you need?

(A) 5¢   (B) 6¢   (C) 7¢   (D) 8¢

Counting Bags

Choose a counting bag.
Record the letter on the bag.
Count the objects in two different ways.

I counted the objects in

Here are the two different ways I counted:

Problems About 2s and 5s (page 1 of 2)

Solve these problems. Show your work.

1. There are 9 children on the playground. How many legs are on the playground?

2. There are 16 arms at the bus stop. How many people are at the bus stop?

Problems About 2s and 5s (page 2 of 2)

3. There are 7 people in the classroom. How many fingers are in the room?

4. There are 80 toes in the swimming pool. How many people are in the pool?

Enough for the Class?

There are 21 students in Ms. Tom's class. Each student needs an eraser. Ms. Tom has 15 erasers.

NOTE Students compare two amounts and find the difference.

1. Are there enough for the class?   YES   NO

2. Are there any extra erasers?   YES   NO

How many? _____

3. Does Ms. Tom need more erasers?   YES   NO

How many? _____

4. How did you figure it out? Use this space to show your work.

Ongoing Review

5. Which coins make 40¢?

(A) 1 nickel and 2 dimes

(B) 2 nickels and 3 dimes

(C) 3 nickels and 2 dimes

(D) 4 nickels and 1 dime

Fingers and Toes at Home

NOTE Students practice counting by groups of 5 and 10.

SMH **35–36, 38, 39**

1. Figure out how many fingers and toes there are in your home. Use numbers and pictures or words to show your thinking.

Can you also use tally marks?

Optional: (Show your work on another sheet of paper.)

2. How many left fingers and toes are there in your family?

3. How many left fingers are in your family?

4. What if you included 3 more people in your count? How many fingers and toes would there be?

Trading Coins

Trade so that you have the fewest possible coins.

NOTE Students practice counting money and finding coin equivalencies.

SMH 19, 20

1. You have 1 quarter, 1 nickel, and 12 pennies. What trade could you make?

2. You have 1 quarter, 3 nickels, and 5 pennies. What trade could you make?

3. You have 1 quarter, 2 dimes, and 1 nickel. What trade could you make?

Ongoing Review

4. How many children were surveyed?

Ⓐ 25   Ⓒ 27

Ⓑ 26   Ⓓ 28

Which sport do you like best?
10 of us like baseball.
8 of us like soccer.
7 of us like football.

Getting to Know Tally Marks

Show the number with tally marks, or count the tallies to find the number.

Example: 7	ⵌ ‖
8	
	ⵌ ⵌ ‖‖
19	
	ⵌ ⵌ ⵌ ⵌ ⵌ ‖‖‖
32	
Choose a number: _____	
Choose a number: _____	

Session 3.7

Grouping by 2s, 5s, and 10s

Our number is _____.

Number in a Tower	Number of Towers	Number of Leftovers	Total Number of Cubes
2			
5			
10			

Our number is _____.

Number in a Tower	Number of Towers	Number of Leftovers	Total Number of Cubes
2			
5			
10			

Our number is _____.

Number in a Tower	Number of Towers	Number of Leftovers	Total Number of Cubes
2			
5			
10			

What Time Is It?

Read each clock. Record what time it is. Record what time it will be in 1 hour.

NOTE Students practice telling time to the hour and half hour and determining and representing the time it will be in one hour.

SMH 139, 141

What time is it now?		What time will it be in one hour?	
	[:]		[:]
	[:]		[:]
	[:]		[:]
	[:]		[:]
	[:]		[:]

Grouping by 10s ✏️

Total Number of Cubes	Number of Towers of 10	Number of Leftovers

What do you notice? Write about any patterns you see. Use another sheet of paper.

Penny-a-Pocket

1. The class gets one penny for every pocket. How many pennies does the class get?

NOTE Students practice addition combinations by solving a problem with several addends. They also practice counting money and finding coin equivalencies.

SMH 20, 43, 46, 54

Students	Number of Pockets	
Howard	4	
Hope	2	
Mike	3	10
Tony	2	
Tamara	0	
Mark	1	
Holly	3	
Sarah	5	
Timothy	7	
Maria	3	
Vipan	1	
Titus	4	
Scott	0	
Hadiya	2	
Harry	6	
Rick	7	
Michelle	4	
Martha	5	
Sean	2	
Thomas	6	

GRAND TOTAL

_____ ¢

2. How could the class trade the pennies for fewer coins?

Problems About 10s and 1s (page 1 of 2)

Solve each problem. Show your work.

1. Sally has 3 towers of 10 connecting cubes and 7 single cubes. How many cubes does Sally have?

2. Jake has 43 connecting cubes. How many towers of 10 can he make? How many leftovers will he have?

Problems About 10s and 1s (page 2 of 2)

3. Franco has 62 pennies. If he trades the pennies for as many dimes as he can, how many dimes will he have? How many pennies will be left?

4. Baseball cards come in packs of 10. Kira has 3 packs and 8 single cards that her brother gave her. How many baseball cards does she have altogether?

More Problems About 10 and 1s (page 1 of 2)

Solve each problem. Show your work.

1. Franco has 76 cards. He is putting them into rows of 10. How many whole rows can he make? How many cards will be left over?

2. Kira has 25¢ in her pocket. If Kira has both dimes and pennies, how many of each coin could she have?

More Problems About 10 and 1s (page 2 of 2)

3. Sally has 4 dimes and 7 pennies in her pocket. How much money does she have?

4. Jake has 6 dimes and 3 pennies in his piggy bank. How much money does he have?

How Much Money?

How much money is in each box?
Write an equation.

NOTE Students practice counting money.

 SMH 19, 20

1.

2.

3.

4.

Ongoing Review

5. If you have 77 pennies, what is the **most** number of dimes you can get in trade?

(A) 6 dimes   (B) 7 dimes   (C) 8 dimes   (D) 11 dimes

How Many Stickers? (page 1 of 2)

1.

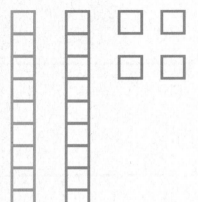

How many stickers? _____

2.

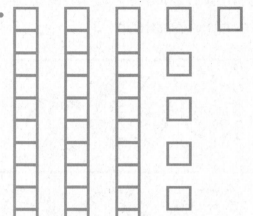

How many stickers? _____

3.

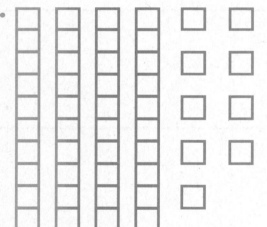

How many stickers? _____

4.

How many stickers? _____

Stickers, Number Strings, and Story Problems

How Many Stickers? (page 2 of 2)

5. Show 21 stickers.

6. Show 17 stickers.

7. Show 33 stickers.

8. Show 46 stickers.

Dimes and Pennies

Solve each problem.
Show your work.

NOTE Students practice solving problems about tens and ones.

SMH 19, 20, 29

1. Kira has 4 dimes and 6 pennies in her pocket. How much money does she have?

2. Jake has 54 pennies . If he trades the pennies for as many dimes as he can, how many dimes will he have? How many pennies?

Ongoing Review

3. Which expression does not make 20?

(A) 20 − 0

(C) 30 − 10

(B) 20 − 20

(D) 40 − 20

46 Stickers

1. Show all of the ways you can make the number 46 with stickers, using only strips of 10, only singles, or both strips and singles.

2. Do you think you have all of the possible combinations? Why do you think that?

Missing Number

NOTE Students practice the doubles and plus 10 addition combinations and sequencing numbers 1–100.

SMH 24, 47

1. Solve these problems and fill in the totals on the 100 chart below.

$7 + 7 =$ _____ $3 + 3 =$ _____ $10 + 2 =$ _____

$9 + 9 =$ _____ $8 + 8 =$ _____ $10 + 8 =$ _____

$4 + 4 =$ _____ $5 + 5 =$ _____ $6 + 10 =$ _____

2. Fill in any other missing numbers on the 100 chart.

1	2	3	4	5		7			
11				15		17		19	
21		23	24	25	26	27	28		30
	32	33	34	35	36	37		39	40
41	42	43	44	45			48	49	
	52	53				57	58		
61	62	63		65		67		69	70
		73	74			77	78	79	80
81	82	83	84		86	87	88	89	
	92	93	94		96	97	98	99	

How Many Stickers?

NOTE Students use place value (tens and ones) to identify and represent numbers.

SMH **28, 29**

1.

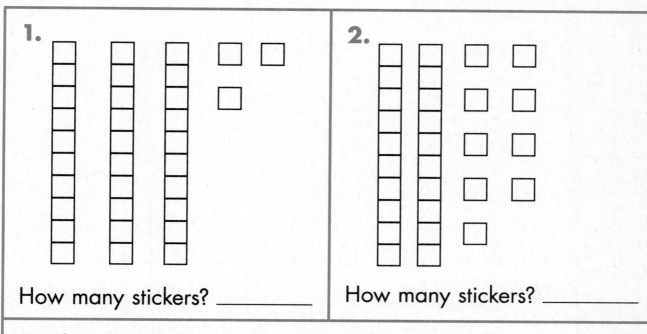

How many stickers? _____

2.

How many stickers? _____

3. Show 78 stickers using strips of 10 and singles.

4. Show all of the possible ways to make 45 with stickers (strips of 10 and singles). Use the back of this page.

Buying Marbles

Tom's Toy Store sells bags of marbles in five different sizes. Here are the number of marbles in each size bag.

NOTE Students find combinations that make a given total.

SMH 76–80

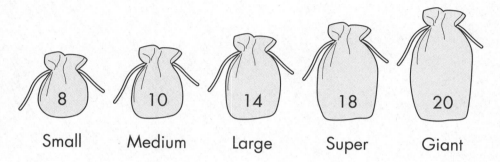

| 8 | 10 | 14 | 18 | 20 |
| Small | Medium | Large | Super | Giant |

Solve each problem. Show your work. Write an equation.

1. Jack bought 2 bags of marbles. He got 28 marbles in all. What size bags could Jack have bought?

2. Mia bought 3 bags of marbles. She got 38 marbles in all. What size bags could Mia have bought?

3. Pam bought some bags of marbles. She got 2 more marbles than Jack and 8 fewer marbles than Mia. How many bags could Pam have bought? What sizes could they have been?

Complicated Kris Northern

"This image illustrates some of the best qualities of fractals—infinity, reiteration, and self similarity."– **Kris Northern**

Investigations
IN NUMBER, DATA, AND SPACE®

Pockets, Teeth, and Favorite Things

Coin Problems

Figure out how much money there is in each box.

Write an equation to show how you counted the money.

NOTE Students practice counting money.

SMH **19, 20**

1.

2.

3.

4.

Guess My Rule Questions

NOTE Students use the given data to figure out additional information.

1. A Grade 2 class was playing *Guess My Rule.* There were 21 students in the class. 8 were wearing stripes. How many students were **not** wearing stripes? Show your work. Write an equation.

2. A Grade 3 class was playing *Guess My Rule.* 6 students were wearing glasses. 18 students were not wearing glasses. How many students were in the class? Show your work. Write an equation.

3. A Grade 2 class was playing *Guess My Rule.* 12 students were wearing sneakers. 10 students were not wearing sneakers. How many **more** students were wearing sneakers? Show your work. Write an equation.

Guess My Rule with Letters

Look closely at the letters that do fit the rule and at the letters that do **not** fit the rule. Then answer the questions.

Fit the Rule	Do Not Fit the Rule
A, E, F, H, I, K, L, M, N	B, C, D, G, J, O, P

1. The rule is _____

2. Write 3 more letters that fit the rule. _____

3. Write 3 more letters that do NOT fit the rule. _____

Ongoing Review

4. The cubes show how many students rode the bus to school today. How many students rode the bus to school?

14 15 16 17
Ⓐ Ⓑ Ⓒ Ⓓ

Story Problems

Solve each problem. Show your work.
Write an equation.

NOTE Students solve two story problems about combining two quantities.

SMH 59, 60, 61

1. Franco had 27 pennies. He found 13 more pennies when he was cleaning his closet. How many pennies does he have?

2. Kira had 21 party hats. She bought 17 more for her party. How many party hats does Kira have now?

Sticker Station Problems

Solve each problem. Show your work.
Write an equation.

NOTE Students use what they know about groups of 10s and 1s to solve story problems.

SMH **27, 28**

1. Franco went to Sticker Station.

He bought 2 strips of 10 and 6 singles of frog stickers. He also bought 5 strips of 10 and 2 singles of butterfly stickers.

How many stickers did Franco buy?

2. Sally also went to Sticker Station.

She bought 3 strips of 10 and 5 singles of skateboard stickers. She also bought 4 strips of 10 and 3 singles of snowman stickers.

How many stickers did Sally buy?

Guess My Rule

Play several games of *Guess My Rule* with a family member or a friend.

> **NOTE** Students have been playing the game "Guess My Rule" with their class. For homework, students play "Guess My Rule" with a family member or a friend. You can play with one rule using the circle or with two rules using the Venn diagram.
>
> **SMH** 108

1. Collect 20 small objects around your home, for example, a pencil, scissors, a paper clip, a stone, a self-stick note, a penny, and other objects.

2. Choose a rule that fits some of the objects.

3. Put two objects that fit your rule in the circle. Put two objects that do **not** fit your rule outside the circle.

4. Your partner does not guess your rule yet. Your partner chooses an object and puts it where he or she thinks it belongs.

5. Tell your partner whether he or she is correct. You should put any misplaced objects where they belong.

6. Repeat steps 4 and 5 until almost all the objects are placed in the circle or outside the circle.

7. Then your partner guesses your rule.

8. Now it is your partner's turn to choose a rule and you play again.

What rules did you use when you played?

1. _____

2. _____

3. _____

4. _____

Sorting Data

Can you help Mr. Murphy's class sort the animals they saw at the zoo into those that fly and those that do **not** fly?

NOTE Students sort and organize a set of data by a given attribute.

bat   rabbit   woodpecker   penguin   frog

lamb   owl   turtle   butterfly   duck

dragonfly   pig   cockroach   horse   cricket

Animals That Fly	**Animals That Do Not Fly**

Analyzing Favorite Things Data ✎ WRITING

Write two things you learned
from your Favorite Things survey:

1. _____

_____

_____

2. _____

_____

_____

Write an equation that shows the results of your survey.

_____

How many people answered your survey? _____

How do you know? _____

_____

_____

_____

Playing *Double It*

Pretend you are playing *Double It*.
Double each card and find the total.
Write an equation.

NOTE Students practice the double combinations.

 SMH **47**

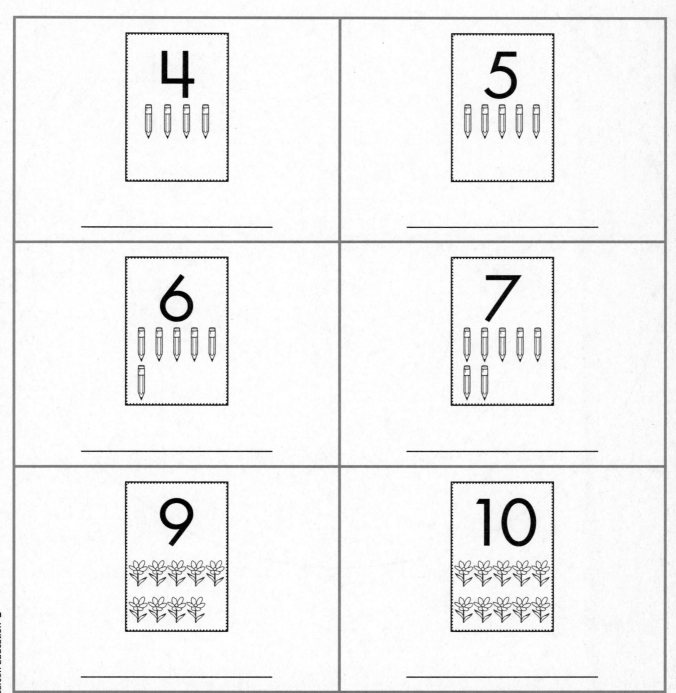

Circle for *Guess My Rule*

Venn Diagram for *Guess My Rule*

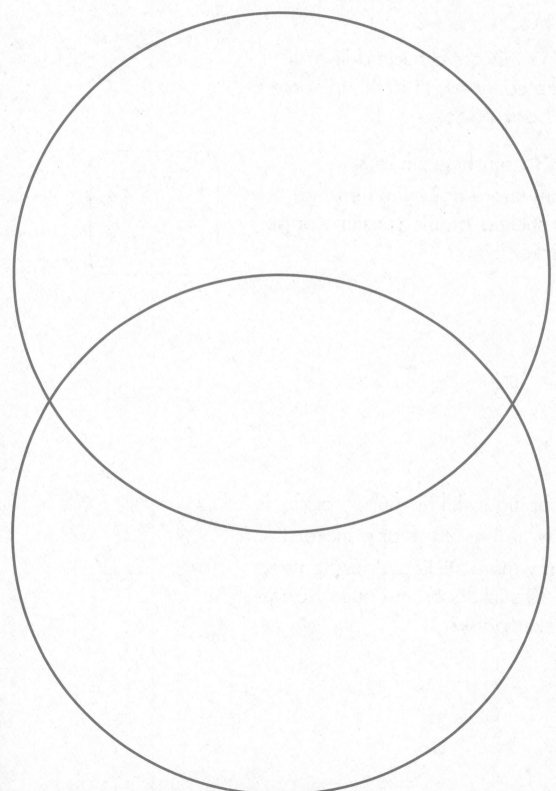

NOTE Students use addition or subtraction to solve 2 story problems.

SMH **79–80**

Even More Sticker Problems

Sticker Station just got a huge delivery! Kira and Jake cannot wait to fill up some of their sticker book pages.

1. Kira has 35 sunshine stickers.

How many more does she need to have 50 stickers on the sunshine page in her sticker book?

2. Jake is hoping to fill his puppy page. Right now he has 28 puppy stickers.

How many more stickers does he need to have 50 stickers on the puppy page in his sticker book?

Guess My Rule
with Two Rules

Guess each rule and write it down.

Rule A   Rule B

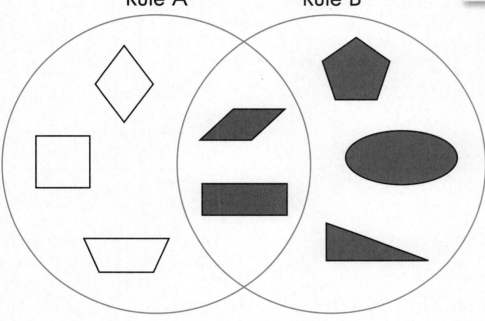

1. Guess Rule A: _____

2. Guess Rule B: _____

3. Draw 1 shape that fits **both** rules.

4. Draw 1 shape that does **not** fit Rule A or Rule B.

Pocket Data from Our Class

Look at the pocket towers you have organized and use them to answer the questions.

1. How many people were wearing 4 pockets? _____

2. What is the most pockets that students had on their clothes today? _____ How many people had this number of pockets? _____

3. What is the fewest pockets that students had on their clothes today? _____ How many people had this number of pockets? _____

4. Circle which is more:

Number of people wearing 6 pockets **OR** Number of people wearing 7 pockets

5. How many pockets did you have on your clothes? _____

6. How many people in the class had more pockets than you did? _____

7. How many people in the class had fewer pockets than you did? _____

8. How many people in the class had the same number of pockets as you did? _____

Playing *Close to 20* (page 1 of 2)

Sally, Jake, and Franco are playing *Close to 20*.
Here is Sally's score sheet.

NOTE Students solve addition number strings and determine how far these sums are from 20.

SMH **54, G2**

Sally's Game Board:

		Total for the Round	Score for the Round
Round 1	7 + 6 + 8	21	1
Round 2	7 + 7 + 3	17	3
Round 3	9 + 0 + 10	19	1
Round 4	10 + 1 + 1	12	8
Round 5	10 + 2 + 8	20	0

Sally's Total Score: 1 + 3 + 1 + 8 + 0 = ___13___

Now fill in Jake's and Franco's score sheets.

Remember that the score for a round is how far the total for that round is from 20. Write an equation to show their total scores.

Playing *Close to 20* (page 2 of 2)

Jake's Game Board:

		Total for the Round	Score for the Round
Round 1	10 + 2 + 5		
Round 2	9 + 9 + 4		
Round 3	6 + 8 + 1		
Round 4	7 + 10 + 2		
Round 5	8 + 2 + 9		

Jake's Total Score: _____

Franco's Game Board:

		Total for the Round	Score for the Round
Round 1	7 + 5 + 3		
Round 2	9 + 7 + 2		
Round 3	10 + 3 + 9		
Round 4	3 + 8 + 7		
Round 5	5 + 10 + 4		

Franco's Total Score: _____

Sorting and Representing Data (page 1 of 2)

Can you help Mr. Murphy's class sort the animals they saw at the zoo into those that fly and those that do **not** fly?

NOTE Students sort and organize a set of data and then make a bar graph.

SMH **106, 107, 109**

bat   rabbit   woodpecker   penguin   frog

lamb   owl   turtle   butterfly   eagle

dragonfly   pig   cockroach   horse   cricket

Animals That Fly	Animals That Do Not Fly

Sorting and Representing Data (page 2 of 2)

Complete the bar graph with the data about the zoo animals.

Title: _____

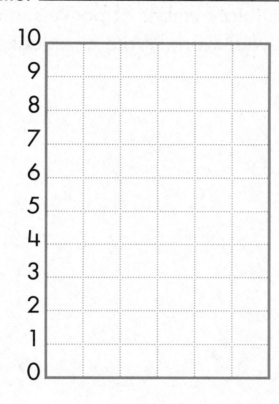

_____ _____

1. How many animals fly? _____

2. Do more animals fly or not fly? _____

3. How many pieces of data are represented on your bar graph? _____

How Many Pockets in All?

1. Fill in a class list with the number of pockets each person is wearing.

2. a. Figure out the total number of pockets in class today. Show your work. Write an equation.

b. Total number of pockets in the class _____

What Time Is It?

Read each clock, and record the time.

NOTE Students practice telling time to the hour and half hour.

 137, 139

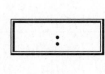

```
:
```

6:30

7:00

```
:
```

8:00

```
:
```

```
:
```

4:30

Our Plan for Collecting Data

Discuss these questions with your partner.
Record your answers.

1. What class willl you collect data from?

_____

2. What will you say to the class to introduce your survey?

_____

_____

_____

3. What question will you ask?

_____

_____

4. How will you keep track of people's answers?

_____

_____

5. How will you make sure you ask everyone the question?

_____

_____

How Many Are Left?

Solve each problem. Show your work.
Write an equation.

NOTE Students solve story problems about subtracting one quantity from another.

SMH 67, 68, 69

1. Sally bought 31 stamps. She used 17 of these stamps to mail her letters to friends. How many stamps does she have left?

2. Franco had 28 baseball cards. He gave 15 of them to Kira. How many baseball cards does he have left?

Trading Card

How Many Teeth?

Survey 2 or 3 of your brothers or sisters, cousins, or friends who are in elementary school to find out how many teeth they have lost. We will use this information during math time.

> **NOTE** Students have been collecting data in class about the total number of teeth students have lost. For homework, students will continue with this type of data collection by asking 2 to 3 other children who are in elementary school how many teeth they have lost.
>
> **SMH** **104, 105**

Name	Grade	Number of Teeth Lost

Looking at a Line Plot

Mr. Fox's students are allowed to check out up to 3 library books. This line plot shows how many books they checked out.

NOTE Students use a line plot to answer questions about and analyze a set of data.

SMH **110, 111**

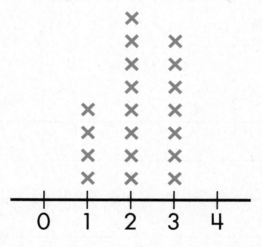

1. How many students checked out 1 book? _____

2. How many students checked out 3 books? _____

3. More students checked out _____ books than any other number of books.

4. Did more students check out 1 book or 3 books? _____

5. How many students are in Mr. Fox's class? _____

How do you know? _____

_____

_____

What Did You Find Out?

Look at your representation of the teeth data you collected from another class.

What do you notice about the number of teeth lost in this class?

Write two things you notice.

1. _____

_____

_____

_____

2. _____

_____

_____

_____

Explaining Someone Else's Findings

1. Who did you trade findings with?

Names: _____ _____

What class did they collect data from? _____

2. What was the most common number of teeth lost? _____

3. What was the fewest and most teeth lost in this class?

Lowest _____ Highest _____

4. How many students lost fewer than 4 teeth? _____

5. How many students lost exactly 4 teeth? _____

6. How many students lost more than 4 teeth? _____

7. How many students were in this class? _____

8. What did you find surprising or unusual in this class's data?

_____

_____

_____

_____

More How Many?

Solve the problem. Show your work.
Write an equation.

NOTE Students practice counting by groups.

SMH 35–36, 37

1. Sally counted 36 feet in her classroom.

How many people were in Sally's classroom?

2. There were 24 kids on the soccer field.

How many feet were there?

Comparing Teeth Data

Look at your representation of the teeth data you collected from another class.
Look at the representation of the teeth data from your own class.

1. How are the number of teeth lost in your class and the number of teeth lost in the other class similar?

2. How are the number of teeth lost in your class and the number of teeth lost in the other class different?

More Coin Problems

Solve each problem.
Show your work.

NOTE Students practice working with groups of 5s and 10s in terms of nickels and dimes.

SMH **19, 20, 38, 39**

1. How many dimes are in 75¢?

2. How many nickels are in 75¢?

3. Sally has 8 nickels and 7 dimes. How much money does she have?

Guess Both of My Rules!

What is the same about the children in each picture?

Can you find the two mystery rules?

> **NOTE** Students guess and record "the rules," or common attributes, of two different groups. They identify pictures that have both of these attributes.

1.

Fits Rule 1	Fits Rule 2

Rule 1 is _____

Rule 2 is _____

2. Circle the children that fit **both** rules.

Mystery Teeth Data: Which Class Is It?

The data in the table show how many teeth each student lost.

Class A		Class B		Class C		Class D	
Alyssa	14	Angel	7	Alfonso	2	Aaron	10
Brian	11	Ayaz	6	Alexandra	2	Allana	11
Danny	8	Bjorn	1	Andrew	1	Ben	5
Daniel	6	Camilla	7	Anthony	0	Botan	8
Evan	8	Chen	3	Brandon	1	Carla	9
Ellie	8	Crystal	13	Britney	1	Chi Wan	12
Erica	9	Ebony	8	Carle	4	Dyala	14
Gordon	8	Franco	6	Clarence	0	Jesse	9
Howard	11	Graham	8	Daniel	1	Julie	14
Karen	13	Harris	9	Eric	0	Kevin	9
Jan	13	Helena	8	Esther	0	Kira	10
Jacob	12	Imani	8	Gordon	3	Laura	7
Lily	7	Jeffrey	9	Grace	0	Liana	8
Maeve	6	Jess	3	Isaac	2	Lois	11
Mary	7	Karina	9	Jackie	0	Lori	12
Maude	8	Laura	12	Jeremiah	3	Morgan	13
Nadeem	5	Lila	8	Jonathan	0	Nat	8
Nadir	7	Linda	8	Katherine	3	Ramon	14
Noah	8	Lionel	5	Latoya	1	Roshma	13
Rachel	8	Naomi	8	Megan	0		
Ricardo	8	Paul	8	Myles	1		
Sarah	8	Samir	9	Ned	3		
Sammy	7	Simon	6	Paul	0		
Tracey	9	Tim	8	Percy	0		
Yanni	8	Tory	8	Yoshi	0		

Mystery Teeth Data: Which Class Is It? Recording Sheet

1. How did you decide which set of Mystery Data went with your representation?

2. What grade level do you think the set of Mystery Data represents, and why?

Representing Data

The survey question was, "How many stuffed animals do you have?"

NOTE Students organize and represent the results of a survey.

SMH 110

Akira	5	Richard	5
Nathan	12	Trevor	4
Kiyo	7	Miranda	11
Leslie	10	Morgan	7
Emily	11	Kyle	7
Mason	6	Becky	9

1. Choose a way to show these data.

Ongoing Review

2. You want 15 counters. How many more do you need?

6
(A)

7
(B)

8
(C)

15
(D)

Organizing Data

Jen's favorite animal is a dog. She loves big dogs and little dogs. She loves dogs with long hair or short hair. She loves dogs that are brown, black or white.

NOTE Students solve real-world problems involving the math content of this unit.

One day at the park, Jen counted 8 dogs. Here are the dogs she saw.

How can Jen sort the dogs?
Think of two rules. Write the rules below.

First way	Second way

What Do You Collect?

Use the bar graph to answer the
questions below.

NOTE Students read and
interpret data from a bar graph.

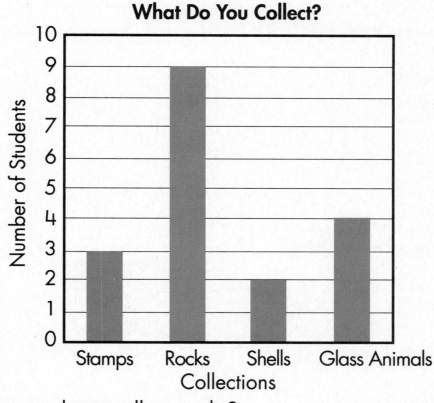

What Do You Collect?

1. How many students collect rocks? _____

2. How many students collect glass animals? _____

3. Compare the number of students who collect shells to the
   number of students who collect rocks.

   a. Which is more? _____

   b. How many more? _____

4. How many students are represented on this graph? _____
   Show how to figure this out.

Complicated Kris Northern

"This image illustrates some of the best qualities of fractals—infinity, reiteration, and self similarity."– **Kris Northern**

Investigations
IN NUMBER, DATA, AND SPACE®

How Many Floors? How Many Rooms?

A Cube Building

1. How many rooms does each floor have? _____

2. If the building has 5 floors, how many rooms are there in the whole building? _____

3. If the building has 10 floors, how many rooms are there in the whole building? _____

4. Show how you figured out how many rooms there are in 10 floors.

Name _____   Date _____

How Many Floors? How Many Rooms?   **Daily Practice**

Close to 20

Sally and Jake are playing *Close to 20*. Fill in Jake's gameboard. The score for a round is how far the total is from 20. Write an equation to show Jake's total score.

> **NOTE** Students solve addition problems and determine the difference between each sum and 20.
>
> **SMH** 54, G2

Sally's Gameboard

		Total	Score
Round 1	4 + 6 + 8	18	2
Round 2	7 + 7 + 3	17	3
Round 3	9 + 0 + 10	19	1
Round 4	10 + 1 + 1	12	8
Round 5	10 + 2 + 8	20	0

Sally's Total Score: 2 + 3 + 1 + 8 + 0 = _____14_____

Jake's Gameboard

		Total	Score
Round 1	5 + 5 + 6		
Round 2	9 + 7 + 3		
Round 3	8 + 8 + 4		
Round 4	7 + 9 + 1		
Round 5	10 + 5 + 2		

Jake's Total Score: _____

Cube Buildings 1

Make one floor of a cube building to fit on the outline. Then build more floors. Fill in the table to show the number of rooms for 1, 2, 3, 4, 5, and 10 floors.

Building A

Total Number of Floors	Total Number of Rooms
1	
2	
3	
4	
5	
10	

Building B

Total Number of Floors	Total Number of Rooms
1	
2	
3	
4	
5	
10	

Cube Buildings 2

Make one floor of a cube building to fit on the outline. Then build more floors. Fill in the table to show the number of rooms for 1, 2, 3, 4, 5, and 10 floors.

Building C

Total Number of Floors	Total Number of Rooms
1	
2	
3	
4	
5	
10	

Building D

Total Number of Floors	Total Number of Rooms
1	
2	
3	
4	
5	
10	

Name   Date

How Many Floors? How Many Rooms?   Daily Practice

Today's Number: 18

Circle all of the problems that equal Today's Number.

NOTE Students determine which expressions are equal to Today's Number.

SMH 55, 56

Today's Number is 18.

$6 + 6 + 3 + 2 + 1$	$28 - 10$
$10 + 8$	$33 - 15$
$5 + 8 + 1$	$4 + 5 + 3 + 6$
$9 + 2 + 6$	$9 + 9$
$25 - 9$	$7 + 8 + 2 + 2 + 1$

Cube Buildings 3

Make one floor of a cube building to fit on the outline. Then build more floors. Fill in the table to show the number of rooms for 1, 2, 3, 4, 5, and 10 floors.

Building E

Total Number of Floors	Total Number of Rooms
1	
2	
3	
4	
5	
10	

Building F

Total Number of Floors	Total Number of Rooms
1	
2	
3	
4	
5	
10	

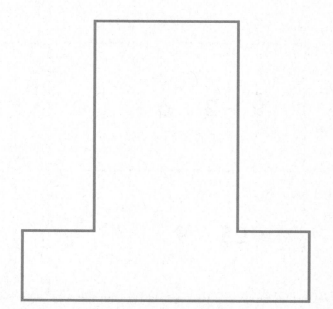

Sessions 1.3, 1.4, 1.5, 1.6

Cube Buildings 4

Make one floor of a cube building to fit on the outline. Then build more floors. Fill in the table to show the number of rooms for 1, 2, 3, 4, 5, and 10 floors.

Building G

Total Number of Floors	Total Number of Rooms
1	
2	
3	
4	
5	
10	

Building H

Total Number of Floors	Total Number of Rooms
1	
2	
3	
4	
5	
10	

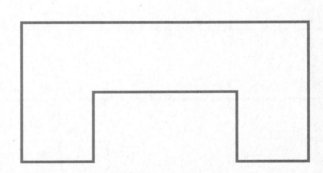

5 Rooms on a Floor

Make some floor plans for buildings
with 5 rooms on each floor.

© Pearson Education 2

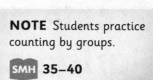

Counting by Groups

Solve each problem. Show your work.
Write an equation.

NOTE Students practice counting by groups.

SMH 35–40

1. There are 23 students in Ms. Lake's class. What is the total number of fingers of all of the students in the class?

2. There are 6 cars in the parking lot. What is the total number of wheels in the parking lot?

3. There is a total of 30 sneakers on people's feet in the classroom. How many people are wearing sneakers?

Ongoing Review

4. Emma made up a rule about buttons.

These buttons do not follow Emma's rule.

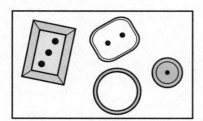

These buttons follow Emma's rule.

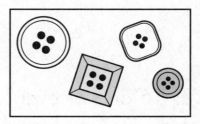

Which one of these buttons follow Emma's rule?

A   B   C   D

Problems About Partners and Teams

NOTE These problems are about even and odd numbers. Students should find their own ways to solve the problem and record the work.

 SMH 41–42

1. a. 17 students are going to lunch. Will everyone have a partner to walk with? Solve the problem. Show your work.

    b. Is 17 odd or even? _____ How do you know?

2. a. There are 16 children who want to play soccer. Can they make two equal teams? Solve the problem. Show your work.

    b. Is 16 odd or even? _____ How do you know?

Floor Plan 1 (page 1 of 2)

Use connecting cubes to build Building I and fill in the missing information in the table. Draw the floor plan below.

Building I	
Total Number of Floors	Total Number of Rooms
1	5
2	
3	15
	20
5	
6	

10	

My Floor Plan

Floor Plan 1 (page 2 of 2)

How did you find out the number of rooms for 5 floors? Show your work.

Floor Plan 2 (page 1 of 2)

Use connecting cubes to build Building J and fill in the missing information in the table. Draw the floor plan below.

Building J	
Total Number of Floors	Total Number of Rooms
2	
3	30
	40
6	60
10	

My Floor Plan

Floor Plan 2 (page 2 of 2)

How did you find out the number of floors for 40 rooms? Show your work.

Floor Plan 3 (page 1 of 2)

Use connecting cubes to build Building K and fill in the missing information in the table. Draw the floor plan below.

Building K	
Total Number of Floors	Total Number of Rooms
1	
	2
3	3
	4
5	
	6

10	

My Floor Plan

Floor Plan 3 (page 2 of 2)

How did you find out the number of rooms for 5 floors? Show your work.

Floor Plan 4 (page 1 of 2)

Use connecting cubes to build Building L and fill in the missing information in the table. Draw the floor plan below.

Building L	
Total Number of Floors	Total Number of Rooms
	3
2	
	9
4	12
6	

10	

My Floor Plan

Floor Plan 4 (page 2 of 2)

How did you find out the number of rooms for 6 floors? Show your work.

Floor Plan 5 (page 1 of 2)

Use connecting cubes to build Building M and fill in the missing information in the table. Draw the floor plan below.

Building M	
Total Number of Floors	Total Number of Rooms
2	4
4	
	12
8	16

10	

My Floor Plan

Floor Plan 5 (page 2 of 2)

How many rooms are on 1 floor of
this building? How do you know?

Floor Plan 6 (page 1 of 2)

Use connecting cubes to build Building N and fill in the missing information in the table. Draw the floor plan below.

Building N	
Total Number of Floors	Total Number of Rooms
2	
	4
6	
	8

10	10

My Floor Plan

Floor Plan 6 (page 2 of 2)

How many rooms are on each floor in this building?
Show your work.

Telling Time to the Hour and Half Hour

Read each clock and write the time.

NOTE Students practice telling time to the hour and the half hour.

SMH 137, 139

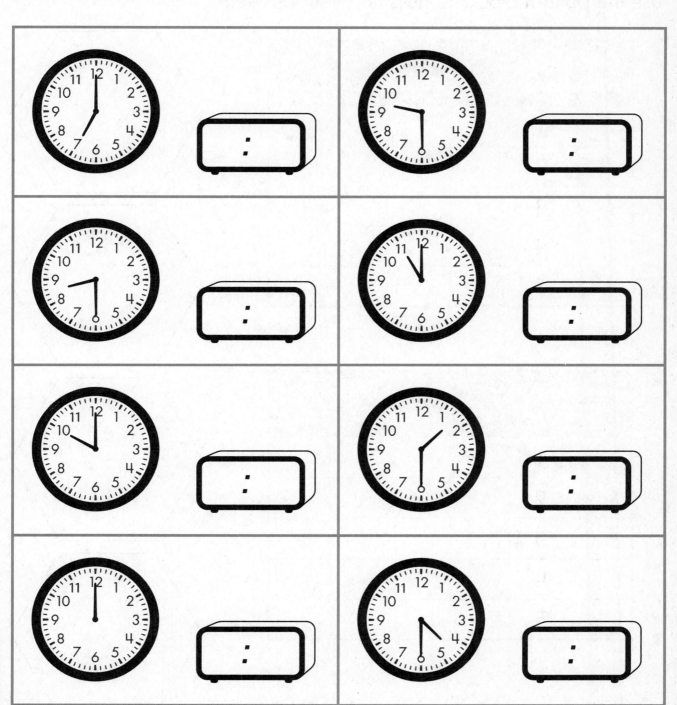

Covering Hexagons

How many of the shape in the second column of each table do you need to cover the hexagons? Use the pattern blocks to help find your answers.

1.

Number of Hexagons ⬡	Number of Rhombuses ▱
1	
2	
3	
4	
5	

2.

Number of Hexagons ⬡	Number of Triangles △
1	
2	
3	
4	
5	

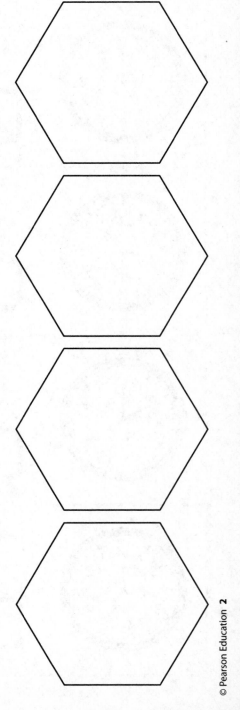

Mystery Shape 1

How many of the mystery shape do you need to cover the rhombus? Use the pattern blocks to help you fill in the rest of the table.

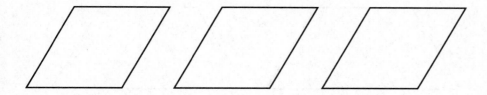

Number of Rhombuses ▱	Number of Mystery Shapes
1	2
2	4
3	
	8
5	10
6	

What is the mystery shape? _____

Mystery Shape 2

How many of the mystery shape do you need to cover the trapezoid? Use the pattern blocks to help you fill in the rest of the table.

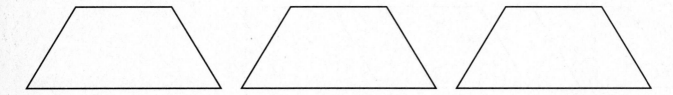

Number of Trapezoids △	Number of Mystery Shapes
1	3
2	
3	
	12
5	15
6	

What is the mystery shape? _____

Mystery Shape 3

How many of the mystery shape do you need to cover the hexagon? Use the pattern blocks to help you fill in the rest of the table.

Number of Hexagons ⬡	Number of Mystery Shapes
1	
2	4
3	
4	8
5	
6	12

What is the mystery shape? _____

Mystery Shape 4

How many of the mystery shape do you need to cover the hexagon? Use the pattern blocks to help you fill in the rest of the table.

Number of Hexagons ⬡	Number of Mystery Shapes
1	
2	6
3	9
5	
6	18

What is the mystery shape? _____

Mystery Shape 5

How many triangles do you need to cover the mystery shape? Use the pattern blocks to help you fill in the rest of the table.

Number of Mystery Shapes	Number of Triangles △
1	
2	12
3	18
4	
5	
6	

What is the mystery shape? _____

Mystery Shape 6

How many triangles do you need to cover the
mystery shape? Use the pattern blocks to help
you fill in the rest of the table.

Number of Mystery Shapes	Number of Triangles △
1	
2	
3	9
4	
5	15
6	

What is the mystery shape? _____

Mystery Shape 7

Find two pattern block shapes that can be Mystery Shape A and Mystery Shape B. Fill in the table.

Number of Mystery Shape A	Number of Mystery Shape B
1	2
2	
3	6
4	
5	10
6	

What is Mystery Shape A? _____

What is Mystery Shape B? _____

Can there be any other answers?

Imagine that the table is about a cube building. Draw a floor plan for that building on a sheet of grid paper.

Mystery Shape 8 ✏️WRITING

Find two pattern block shapes that can be Mystery Shape A and Mystery Shape B. Fill in the table.

Number of Mystery Shape A	Number of Mystery Shape B
	3
3	9
	12
5	15
6	

What is Mystery Shape A? _____

What is Mystery Shape B? _____

Can there be any other answers?

Imagine that the table is about a cube building. Draw a floor plan for that building on a sheet of grid paper.

Addition Combinations

1. Solve these problems. Fill in the totals on the 100 chart below.

NOTE Students practice solving addition combinations and sequencing numbers 1–100.

SMH 24, 25, 54

$5 + 4 + 3 + 1 + 2 =$ _____ $2 + 2 + 10 + 10 =$ _____

$2 + 8 + 7 + 7 + 3 =$ _____ $7 + 3 + 7 + 2 =$ _____

$6 + 6 + 8 + 2 + 4 =$ _____ $5 + 10 + 3 + 10 =$ _____

2. Fill in the other missing numbers on the 100 chart.

	2	3	4	5	6	7	8	9	
11			14		16	17	18		20
21	22	23		25					
		33		35		37		39	
41	42		44	45	46		48	49	
	52	53				57	58	59	
61	62	63		65		67	68	69	70
		73			76			79	80
	82	83	84	85	86	87	88	89	
	92	93			96	97	98		100

Cube Buildings (page 1 of 2)

Solve each problem. Show your work.
Write an equation.

> **NOTE** Students solve addition and subtraction story problems where the starting amount is unknown.

1. a. Jake made the first part of a cube building. He then added on 25 cubes. Now his building has 50 cubes. How many cubes did Jake start with? _____

b. If Jake's building had 50 cubes in all and there were 5 rooms (cubes) on each floor of his building, how many floors are in Jake's building? _____

Cube Buildings (page 2 of 2)

Solve each problem. Show your work. Write an equation.

2. Kira built a cube building. She decided to take off 22 cubes. When she recounted, her building only had 14 cubes. How many cubes did Kira start with? _____

3. Kira and Jake decided to make a cube building together. Kira built the first part of the building and then Jake added on 42 cubes. When they finished, they counted 60 cubes in all. How many cubes were in Kira's part of the building? _____

Pairs of Socks

1. Jake has 10 pairs of new socks. Fill in the table to find the total number of socks he has.

NOTE Students identify the relationship between two quantities to complete the table.

SMH 96, 97–98

Pairs of Socks	
Number of Pairs	Total Number of Socks
1	2
2	
3	
4	
5	

10	

Ongoing Review

2. 10 + _____ = 11

21	10	2	1
Ⓐ	Ⓑ	Ⓒ	Ⓓ

How Many Flowers?

Solve the problem. Show your work.
Write an equation.

> **NOTE** Students solve story problems in which one part is unknown. Students should find their own ways to solve each problem and record the work.
>
> **SMH** 76, 77

1. Kira had 28 flowers. Sally gave her some more. Now Kira has 43 flowers. How many flowers did Sally give to Kira?

2. Sally gave Franco 27 flowers. Franco picked some more flowers. At the end of the day, Franco had 49 flowers. How many flowers did Franco pick?

3. There were 22 flowers in the vase. Jake put in some more flowers. Now there are 37 flowers in the vase. How many flowers did Jake put into the vase?

Cube Patterns

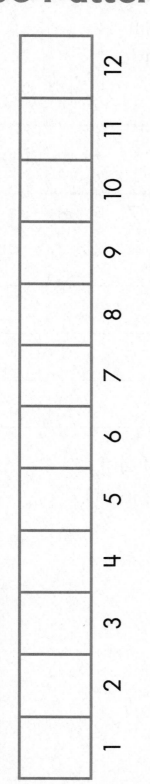

1. Make a pattern with the cubes. Then color it in below.

1 2 3 4 5 6 7 8 9 10 11 12

2. Make another pattern with the cubes. Then color it in below.

1 2 3 4 5 6 7 8 9 10 11 12

Cube Train Pattern A

Build a **red–blue–red–blue** pattern train with
8 cubes. Color in the pattern on the number strip,
and answer the questions below.

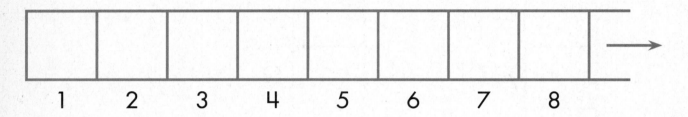

1. What color is the 3rd cube? _____

2. What color is the 6th cube? _____

3. What color is the 10th cube? _____

4. What color is the 13th cube? _____

5. **a.** Look at all the cubes that are **blue** and write
their numbers. Keep going until you get to 20.

b. Write one thing you notice about the
number pattern.

Packs of Juice Boxes

NOTE Students identify the relationship between two quantities to complete the table.

SMH 96, 97–98

1. Jake and Sally need to buy packs of juice boxes for their soccer team. One pack has 6 juice boxes. Use the information below to fill in the table.

Packs of Juice Boxes	
Number of Packs	Total Number of Juice Boxes
1	
2	
3	
	24
5	
10	

Ongoing Review

2. Which numbers are missing in the counting strip?

28, 29   29, 30   30, 31   31, 32

 Ⓐ   Ⓑ   Ⓒ   Ⓓ

| 28 |
| 29 |
| — |
| — |
| 32 |

Cube Train Pattern B (page 1 of 2)

Build a **yellow–red–blue** pattern train with
9 cubes. Color in the pattern on the number strip,
and answer the questions below.

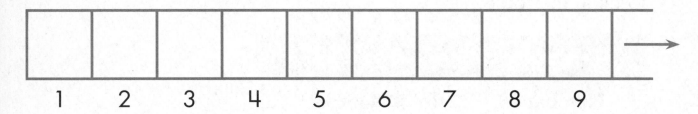

1	2	3	4	5	6	7	8	9

1. What color is the 3rd cube? _____

2. What color is the 6th cube? _____

3. What color is the 10th cube? _____

4. What color is the 12th cube? _____

5. a. Look at all the cubes that are **blue** and write
their numbers. Keep going until you get to 30.

b. Write one thing you notice about the number pattern.

Cube Train Pattern B (page 2 of 2)

6. a. Look at all the cubes that are **yellow** and write their numbers. Keep going until you get past 30.

b. Write one thing you notice about the number pattern. How is it different from or similar to the list for the **blue** cubes?

7. a. Look at all the cubes that are **red** and write their numbers. Keep going until you get past 30.

b. Write one thing you notice about the number pattern. How is it different from or similar to the list for the **blue** cubes?

Name _____ Date _____

How Many Floors? How Many Rooms? Daily Practice

Addition and Subtraction Equations

NOTE Students solve addition and subtraction equations.

SMH 54

Solve these problems.

1.

$8 + 8 + 2 + 3 = $ _____

2.

$9 + 8 + 10 + 9 = $ _____

3.

$17 - 4 - 6 - 3 = $ _____

4.

$7 + 6 + 6 + 5 = $ _____

5.

$22 - 7 + 8 = $ _____

6.

$6 + 9 - 5 - 10 = $ _____

7.

$13 - 8 + 5 = $ _____

8.

$14 + 16 + 5 + 5 = $ _____

9.

$10 - 7 + 3 + 3 = $ _____

10.

$4 + 5 + 4 + 4 = $ _____

11.

$6 + 5 + 4 + 3 + 2 = $ _____

12.

$1 + 10 + 2 + 0 = $ _____

How Much Money?

How much money is in each box?

Write an equation in each box to show how you counted the money.

> **NOTE** For each problem, students determine the amount of money, and then write an equation to show how they counted the money.
>
> **SMH** 19, 20

1.

2.

3.

4.

Cube Train Pattern C

Build a **yellow–yellow–green–green–orange**
pattern train with 10 cubes. Color in the pattern on
the number strip, and answer the questions below.

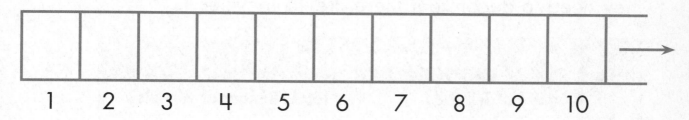

1   2   3   4   5   6   7   8   9   10

1. What color is the 5th cube? _____

2. What color is the 10th cube? _____

3. a. If you were going to keep the pattern going,
   what number would the next **orange** cube be? _____

    b. What number would the next
   orange cube be after that? _____

4. a. Write the numbers matched with **orange**
   cubes. Keep going until you get to 50.

    b. Write one thing you notice about the number pattern.

Name _____ Date _____

How Many Floors? How Many Rooms?   Daily Practice

Tricycle Wheels

NOTE Students identify the relationship between two quantities to complete the table.

 96, 97–98

1. Franco and Kira are decorating tricycle wheels for their neighborhood parade. Fill in the table to find how many wheels they need to decorate if there are 15 tricycles.

Tricycle Wheels	
Number of Tricycles	**Total Number of Wheels**
1	3
2	
3	
4	
5	

10	
11	
12	

15	

Ongoing Review

2. Which shows a combination of 12?

6 + 9	7 + 5	3 + 8	5 + 5
Ⓐ	Ⓑ	Ⓒ	Ⓓ

Transportation Data (page 1 of 2)

NOTE Students represent a set of data on a bar graph and then answer questions about the data.

Mr. Brown's 2nd-grade class took a survey about how students got to school each morning. This is what they found out:

Bike: 5 students
Car: 8 students
Bus: 12 students
Walk: 4 students

1. Make a bar graph that shows the data from Mr. Brown's class.

How Students Get to School

Number of Students

Transportation Data (page 2 of 2)

2. What could be the title of this graph?

_____

3. Do more students ride the bus or ride their bikes?

_____

4. How many more students come by car than walk?

_____

5. How many students responded to this survey?

_____

6. Write two facts about this data set.

_____

_____

_____

_____

Cube Train Pattern D (page 1 of 3)

1. Build a **red-blue-brown-green** pattern with
   8 cubes. Color in the pattern on the number
   strip, and answer the questions below.

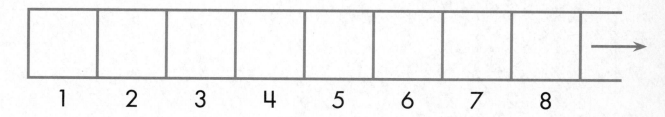

If you keep the pattern going,
what color will the 12th cube be? _____

What number will the next **green** cube be? _____

Look at all the cubes that are **green** and write
their numbers. Keep going until you get to 40.

Cube Train Pattern D (page 2 of 3)

2. Build a **yellow–black–white–orange** pattern train with 8 cubes. Color in the pattern on the number strip, and answer the questions below.

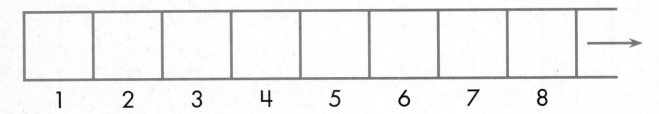

1   2   3   4   5   6   7   8

If you keep the pattern going, what color will the 12th cube be? _____

What number will the next **orange** cube be? _____

Look at all the cubes that are **orange** and write their numbers. Keep going until you get to 40.

Cube Train Pattern D (page 3 of 3)

3. Look at the **red–blue–brown–green** pattern
and the **yellow–black–white–orange** pattern.
What is the same and what is different?

4. Build another cube pattern that will give you a 4,
8, 12, . . . pattern for one of the colors. Color in
your new pattern on the number strip below.

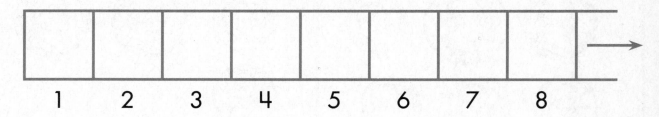

1	2	3	4	5	6	7	8

Which color will be in the 4th, 8th, 12th,
and 16th squares if the pattern keeps going? _____

How Much Money?

How much money is in each box?

Write an equation in each box to show
how you counted the money.

NOTE Students practice
counting money.

SMH 19, 20

1.

2.

3.

4.

How Many Stickers?

NOTE Students use their understanding about groups of 10s and 1s to determine the number of stickers in a set and solve sticker problems.

SMH 27, 28

1.

How many stickers? _____

2.

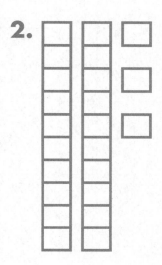

How many stickers? _____

3.

How many stickers? _____

4.

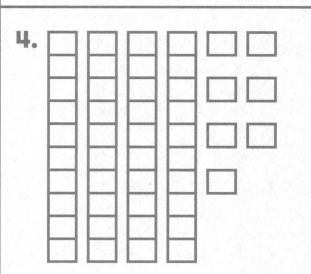

How many stickers? _____

NOTE Students use ratios in a real-life situation.

Bake a Cake

Franco is baking a fruitcake. Here is a list of the ingredients that Franco will use for one fruitcake.

1 cup chopped pineapple   4 tablespoons chopped almonds

2 cups coconut $\frac{1}{2}$ cup milk

3 cups of flour   6 eggs

1. How many cups of pineapple does Franco need for 2 fruitcakes?

2. Franco decides to make 4 fruitcakes. How many eggs does he need?

3. Franco's friend Kira will make 3 fruitcakes. How many cups of coconut will she need?

4. Franco has five cups of flour. Does he have enough flour to make 2 fruitcakes?

5. How many cups of milk will Franco need if he wants to bake 4 fruitcakes?

Complicated Kris Northern

"This image illustrates some of the best qualities of fractals—infinity, reiteration, and self similarity."– **Kris Northern**

Investigations
IN NUMBER, DATA, AND SPACE®

How Many Tens? How Many Ones?

Investigation 5A

Sticker Problems (page 1 of 2)

Solve each problem. Show your work and write an equation.

1. Sally went to Sticker Station. She bought 2 strips of ten star stickers and 6 single star stickers. She also bought 2 strips of ten moon stickers and 3 single moon stickers. How many stickers did Sally buy?

2. Franco had 25 dragon stickers. He went to Sticker Station and bought 2 more strips of ten dragon stickers. How many stickers does Franco have now?

Sticker Problems (page 2 of 2)

3. Jake bought some stickers at Sticker Station. He bought 4 strips of ten sun stickers and 3 single sun stickers. He also bought 2 strips of ten moon stickers and 5 single moon stickers. How many stickers did Jake buy?

4. Kira had 30 puppy stickers. She went to Sticker Station and bought one more strip of ten puppy stickers and 5 single puppy stickers. How many stickers does Kira have now?

Telling Time Problems

Read each clock. Record what time it is. Also record what time it will be in two hours. Write each time three ways.

NOTE Students practice telling and determining time to the hour and the half hour.

SMH **137, 139, 141**

What time is it now?	What time will it be in two hours?
: eight o'clock	: _____
: five thirty	: _____
2:30 two thirty	: _____
: _____	: _____
10:00	: _____

More Sticker Problems (page 1 of 2)

Solve each problem. Show your work and write an equation.

1. Jake had 36 circus stickers. He gave 10 to his sister and 10 to a friend. How many circus stickers does Jake have left?

2. Franco had 62 wizard stickers. He gave 3 strips of ten and 2 singles to Jake. How many wizard stickers does Franco have left?

More Sticker Problems (page 2 of 2)

3. Sally had 44 moon stickers. Before dinner she put 3 strips of ten in her sticker book. How many moon stickers does Sally have left to put in her book?

4. Kira had 58 car stickers. She gave 2 strips of ten and 4 singles to her brother. How many car stickers does Kira have left?

Today's Number with Coins

Today's Number is <u>53</u>.

NOTE Students write expressions that equal Today's Number, using values of coins. There are many possible solutions.

 SMH **19, 55, 57**

> 25¢ + 25¢ + 1¢ + 1¢ + 1¢
>
> 25¢ + 25¢ + 5¢ − 1¢ − 1¢
>
> 25¢ + 10¢ + 10¢ + 5¢ + 1¢ + 1¢ + 1¢

Write at least 5 different ways to make Today's Number with coins. Use pennies, nickels, dimes, or quarters.

Story Problems (page 1 of 2)

Solve each problem. Show your work and write an equation.

1. Franco had 27 kite stickers. He went to Sticker Station and bought 3 more strips of ten. How many stickers does Franco have now?

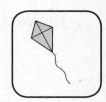

2. On Saturday, Kira and Jake counted animals in the park. They counted 23 pigeons and 37 squirrels. How many animals did they count?

Story Problems (page 2 of 2)

3. Sally had 64 bunny stickers. She gave 2 strips of ten and 3 singles to Franco. How many bunny stickers does Sally have left?

4. Mrs. Brown had 59 pencils. She gave 32 of them to Mr. Blue to borrow. How many pencils does Mrs. Brown have left?

Cat Stickers and Jumping Rope

NOTE Students use addition or subtraction to solve story problems.

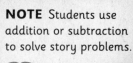 **62–64, 70–72**

Solve each problem. Show your work and write an equation.

1. Sally had 57 cat stickers. She gave 3 strips of ten cat stickers and 5 single cat stickers to Kira. How many cat stickers does Sally have now?

2. Franco and Jake were jumping rope. Franco counted 34 jumps. Jake counted 22 jumps. How many jumps did they count in all?

Ongoing Review

3. Which shape does **not** belong in this group?

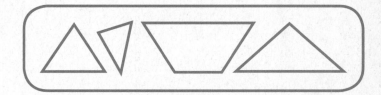

Ⓐ

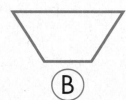
Ⓑ

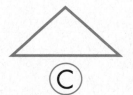
Ⓒ

Ⓓ

Sticker Problems at Home (page 1 of 2)

NOTE Students solve problems about Sticker Station, a store that sells stickers in strips of 10 and individually as singles. These problems focus on place value and adding 10s and 1s.

SMH **28, 32, 63–64**

Write an equation. Then solve the problem and show your work.

1. Franco went to Sticker Station. He bought 1 strip of ten sun stickers and 5 single sun stickers. He also bought 2 strips of ten moon stickers and 1 single moon sticker. How many stickers did Franco buy?

2. Sally collects sports stickers. At Sticker Station she bought 1 strip of ten soccer stickers and 2 single soccer stickers. She also bought 3 strips of ten basketball stickers and 2 single basketball stickers. How many stickers did Sally buy?

Sticker Problems at Home (page 2 of 2)

3. Jake collects animal stickers. At Sticker Station he bought 2 strips of ten bird stickers and 3 single bird stickers. He also bought 1 strip of ten fish stickers and 4 single fish stickers. How many stickers did Jake buy?

4. Kira went to Sticker Station. She bought 3 strips of ten kite stickers and 1 single kite sticker. She also bought 1 strip of ten car stickers and 7 single car stickers. How many stickers did Kira buy?

More Story Problems (page 1 of 2)

Solve each problem. Show your work and write an equation.

1. Sally had 67 pennies. She used 41 of them to buy a glitter pen. How many pennies does she have left?

2. Franco had 43 stamps in his collection. His mother gave him 39 more stamps. How many stamps does Franco have now?

More Story Problems (page 2 of 2)

3. Kira and Sally made 53 snowballs for the big snowball fight. They threw 21 snowballs. How many snowballs do they have left?

4. Jake found 28 marbles in his closet. He bought 54 more marbles at the store. How many marbles does Jake have now?

Close to 20 Problems

Sally and Jake are playing *Close to 20*.
Fill in the rest of Jake's sheet.

Remember: The score for a round is how far
the total for that round is from 20.

> **NOTE** Students solve
> addition problems with
> 3 addends and determine
> how far the totals are
> from 20.
>
> **SMH** 54, G2

Sally's Gameboard:

		Total	Score
Round 1	4 + 6 + 8	18	2
Round 2	10 + 9 + 3	22	2
Round 3	9 + 0 + 10	19	1
Round 4	10 + 1 + 1	12	8
Round 5	10 + 2 + 8	20	0

Sally's Total Score: 2 + 2 + 1 + 8 + 0 = ____13____

Jake's Gameboard:

		Total	Score
Round 1	9 + 5 + 7		
Round 2	8 + 7 + 3		
Round 3	10 + 7 + 7		
Round 4	6 + 6 + 8		
Round 5	7 + 9 + 3		

Jake's Total Score: _____

How Many Tens? How Many Ones?

Mini 100 Charts

1	2	3	4	5	6	7	8	9	10
11	12	13	14	15	16	17	18	19	20
21	22	23	24	25	26	27	28	29	30
31	32	33	34	35	36	37	38	39	40
41	42	43	44	45	46	47	48	49	50
51	52	53	54	55	56	57	58	59	60
61	62	63	64	65	66	67	68	69	70
71	72	73	74	75	76	77	78	79	80
81	82	83	84	85	86	87	88	89	90
91	92	93	94	95	96	97	98	99	100

1	2	3	4	5	6	7	8	9	10
11	12	13	14	15	16	17	18	19	20
21	22	23	24	25	26	27	28	29	30
31	32	33	34	35	36	37	38	39	40
41	42	43	44	45	46	47	48	49	50
51	52	53	54	55	56	57	58	59	60
61	62	63	64	65	66	67	68	69	70
71	72	73	74	75	76	77	78	79	80
81	82	83	84	85	86	87	88	89	90
91	92	93	94	95	96	97	98	99	100

1	2	3	4	5	6	7	8	9	10
11	12	13	14	15	16	17	18	19	20
21	22	23	24	25	26	27	28	29	30
31	32	33	34	35	36	37	38	39	40
41	42	43	44	45	46	47	48	49	50
51	52	53	54	55	56	57	58	59	60
61	62	63	64	65	66	67	68	69	70
71	72	73	74	75	76	77	78	79	80
81	82	83	84	85	86	87	88	89	90
91	92	93	94	95	96	97	98	99	100

1	2	3	4	5	6	7	8	9	10
11	12	13	14	15	16	17	18	19	20
21	22	23	24	25	26	27	28	29	30
31	32	33	34	35	36	37	38	39	40
41	42	43	44	45	46	47	48	49	50
51	52	53	54	55	56	57	58	59	60
61	62	63	64	65	66	67	68	69	70
71	72	73	74	75	76	77	78	79	80
81	82	83	84	85	86	87	88	89	90
91	92	93	94	95	96	97	98	99	100

How Many Tens? How Many Ones?   Daily Practice

The 100 Chart

Fill in the missing numbers to complete the chart.

NOTE Students practice sequencing numbers from 1 to 100.

SMH **24, 25**

	2	3	4			7	8	9	
	12	13	14			17	18	19	
	22	23	24			27	28	29	
	32	33	34			37	38	39	
	42	43	44			47	48	49	
	62	63	64			67	68	69	
	72	73	74			77	78	79	
	82	83	84			87	88	89	
	92	93	94			97	98	99	

Name   Date

How Many Tens? How Many Ones?   **Daily Practice**

The 100 Chart and Sticker Problems

> **NOTE** Students solve addition and subtraction story problems where the starting amount is unknown.

Solve each problem. Show your work. Write an equation.

1. Leo bought sun stickers at Sticker Station. He also bought 21 moon stickers. He bought 36 stickers in all. How many sun stickers did Leo buy?

2. Amaya bought cat stickers at Sticker Station. She gave 13 of them to Leo and kept 32 for herself. How many cat stickers did Amaya buy?

More Sticker Problems at Home (page 1 of 2)

Solve each problem. Show your work and write an equation.

NOTE Students solve problems about Sticker Station, a store that sells stickers in strips of 10 and individually as singles. These problems focus on addition, subtraction, and place value (10s and 1s).

SMH **62–64, 70–72**

1. Kira bought 64 cat stickers from Sticker Station. She gave 2 strips of ten to Franco. How many cat stickers did Kira have left?

2. Sally went to Sticker Station to buy stickers. She bought 3 strips of ten balloon stickers and 3 single balloon stickers. She also bought 2 strips of ten puppy stickers and 4 single puppy stickers. How many stickers did Sally buy?

More Sticker Problems at Home (page 2 of 2)

3. Jake went to Sticker Station. He bought 4 strips of ten train stickers and 1 single train sticker. He also bought 2 strips of ten flower stickers and 6 single flower stickers. How many stickers did Jake buy?

4. Franco had 5 strips of ten baseball stickers and 9 single baseball stickers. He gave two strips of ten and 7 singles to Sally. How many baseball stickers did Franco have left?

Name _____ Date _____

How Many Tens? How Many Ones?   Daily Practice

Exploring the 100 Chart

NOTE Students practice sequencing numbers from 1 to 100.

SMH 24, 25

1	2	3	4	5	6	7	8	9	10
11	12	13	14	15	16	17	18	19	20
21	22	23	24	25	26	27	28	29	30
31	32	33	34	35	36	37	38	39	40
41	42	43	44	45	46	47	48	49	50
51	52	53	54	55	56	57	58	59	60
61	62	63	64	65	66	67	68	69	70
71	72	73	74	75	76	77	78	79	80
81	82	83	84	85	86	87	88	89	90
91	92	93	94	95	96	97	98	99	100

Look at the highlighted numbers. What patterns do you notice?

_____

_____

_____

_____

Fill in the missing numbers.

1.

				55			59	
				65			69	

2.

				85			89	
				95			99	

Ongoing Review

3. Which addition or subtraction combination does **not** make 100?

(A) 101 − 1   (B) 99 + 1   (C) 98 + 2   (D) 98 − 2

Missing Numbers (page 1 of 2)

	2								
				25					
									60
						87			
91									

Fill in the following numbers on the 100 chart and explain how you figured out where they go.

20 _____

3 _____

75 _____

43 _____

Missing Numbers (page 2 of 2)

				5					
21									
					47				
	63								
								90	

39 _____

85 _____

8 _____

70 _____

Missing Numbers Problems

NOTE Students practice solving addition combinations and sequencing numbers from 1 to 100.

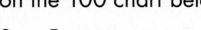 **24, 25**

1. Solve these problems. Fill in the totals on the 100 chart below.

3 + 5 = _____	8 + 3 = _____	4 + 9 = _____
9 + 10 = _____	8 + 4 = _____	8 + 6 = _____
7 + 9 = _____	5 + 0 = _____	6 + 9 = _____
5 + 5 = _____	0 + 3 = _____	2 + 7 = _____

2. Fill in the other missing numbers on the 100 chart.

1	2		4		6	7			
							17	18		20
21	22	23		25	26				
		33		35		37		39	
41	42		44	45	46		48	49	50
	52	53				57	58	59	
61	62		64	65		67	68	69	
71		73	74		76			79	80
	82	83	84	85		87	88	89	90
91		93		95	96			99	

How Many Cubes? (page 1 of 2)

Solve each problem. Show your work and write an equation.

NOTE Students solve addition and subtraction problems about the game "Roll-a-Square."

SMH **60, 68**

1. Jake and Sally were playing *Roll-a-Square*. They had 27 cubes and then rolled a 9. How many cubes do they have now?

2. Kira and Franco were playing *Roll-a-Square*. They had just received 53 cubes, but they landed on the space that says "Oh No! Give back 6 cubes." How many cubes do they have now?

How Many Cubes? (page 2 of 2)

3. Jake and Franco were playing *Roll-a-Square*.
They had 46 cubes and then landed on the
space that says "Great! Take 5 more cubes."
How many cubes do they have now?

4. Sally and Kira were playing *Roll-a-Square*. They
had 54 cubes and then rolled a 7. How many
cubes do they have now?

Sticker Books (page 1 of 4)

Kira collected stickers for a very long time. She kept many strips and singles of different kinds of stickers in a shoebox. When Kira wanted to look at her stickers, she had to spread them out on the floor. One day Kira went to Sticker Station and she noticed something new: Sticker Books! Each book had 10 pages, and on each page there were 10 rows with pockets for holding stickers. Each row could hold either one strip of 10 stickers or 10 single stickers. At the bottom of each page was a place to write what kind of stickers are on the page. The Sticker Books looked like this:

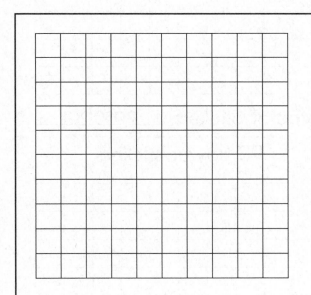

Type of Sticker: _____

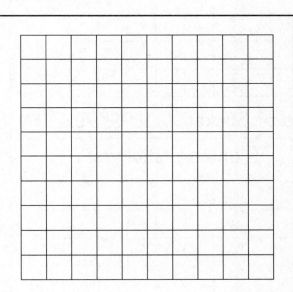

Type of Sticker: _____

Kira was so excited! Finally, she could organize and keep track of all her stickers! She bought a book and rushed home to get to work.

Sticker Books (page 2 of 4)

Show what the pages in Kira's Sticker Book would look like if she had the following:

46 ocean stickers

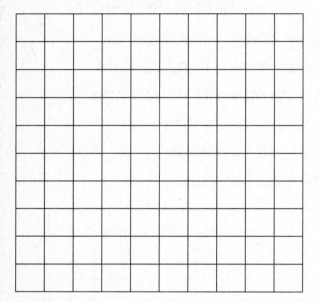

Type of Sticker: _____ocean_____

61 baseball stickers

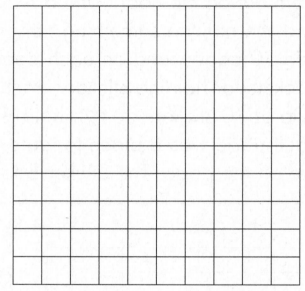

Type of Sticker: _____baseball_____

75 unicorn stickers

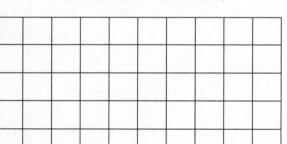

Type of Sticker: _____unicorn_____

98 flower stickers

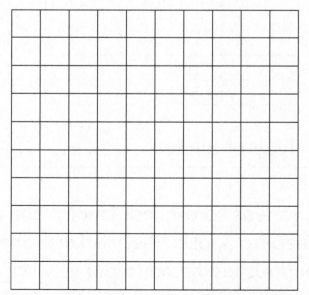

Type of Sticker: _____flower_____

Sticker Books (page 3 of 4)

Solve the problems. Show your work. You can use the grids you colored in on page 28 to help you.

1. Kira has 46 ocean stickers. How many more ocean stickers does Kira need to have 70 ocean stickers?

2. Kira has 61 baseball stickers. How many more baseball stickers does Kira need to have 80 baseball stickers?

Sticker Books (page 4 of 4)

3. Kira has 75 unicorn stickers. How many more unicorn stickers does Kira need to have 85 unicorn stickers?

4. Kira has 98 flower stickers. Kira found 12 more flower stickers. How many flower stickers does Kira have now?

Ten Rows of Ten

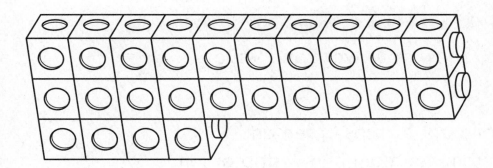

NOTE Students use addition or subtraction to find the difference between a number and a multiple of 10.

SMH 46, 78–80

1. How many more cubes do you need to finish another row of 10? _____

2. Start with the cubes shown. How many more cubes do you need to reach 50? _____

3. Start with the cubes shown. How many more cubes do you need to reach 100? _____

Ongoing Review

4. There are 4 apples in a basket.
Gina puts 7 more apples in the basket.
How many apples are in the basket now?

4	7	10	11
Ⓐ	Ⓑ	Ⓒ	Ⓓ

5. What is the sum of the dots on the dot cubes?

12	10	9	8
Ⓐ	Ⓑ	Ⓒ	Ⓓ

How Many Stickers?
How Many Points? (page 1 of 2)

Solve each problem. Show your work and write
an equation.

1. For a present, Sally got 5 strips of ten and
3 single stickers from her mom and 1 strip of ten
and 7 single stickers from her dad. How many
stickers does Sally have in all?

2. Jake went to Sticker Station and bought 3 strips
of ten cat stickers and 6 single cat stickers. He
also bought 3 strips of ten dog stickers and
4 single dog stickers. How many stickers
did Jake buy?

How Many Stickers?
How Many Points? (page 2 of 2)

3. Franco and Kira are on the same basketball team. At the last game, they each scored 36 points. How many points did Kira and Franco score for their team?

4. Jake and Sally are on the same basketball team. At the last game, Sally scored 43 points and Jake scored 24 points. How many points did Jake and Sally score for their team?

Solving a Sticker Problem

NOTE Students use addition or subtraction to find the difference between a number and a multiple of 10.

SMH 78–80

Solve the problem. Show your work. Write an equation.

Sally had 27 airplane stickers.

How many more does she need to have 40?

What Time Is It?

1. Count the minutes on the clock by groups of 5. Label each group of 5.

NOTE Students label a clock and practice telling time in 5—minute intervals.

SMH 136–138

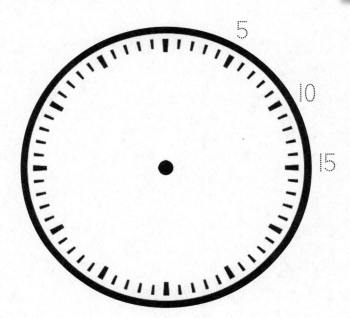

Read each clock. Record what time it is.

2. 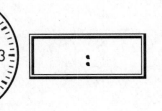 ☐ : ☐

3.  ☐ : ☐

4. 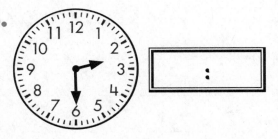 ☐ : ☐

5.  ☐ : ☐

How Many More? (page 1 of 2)

Use the grids to solve the problems.
Write an equation.

NOTE Students solve problems that involve finding a missing part.

SMH 28, 78–80

1. Sally has 37 surfing stickers. Color in the grid to show how many surfing stickers Sally has.

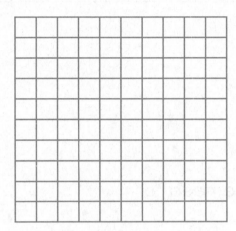

Equation:

_____

How many more surfing stickers does Sally need to have 60 surfing stickers?

2. Jake collects bird stickers. How many bird stickers does Jake have? _____

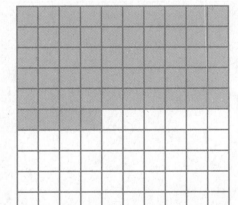

Equation:

_____

How many more does he need to have 80 bird stickers?

How Many More? (page 2 of 2)

3. Jake has 53 fish stickers. Color in the grid to show how many fish stickers Jake has.

Equation:

_____

How many more fish stickers does Jake need to have 90 fish stickers?

4. Sally is collecting dragon stickers. How many dragon stickers does Sally have? _____

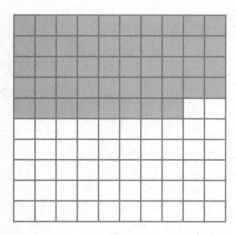

Equation:

_____

How many more does she need to have 95 dragon stickers?

Name _____ Date _____

How Many Tens? How Many Ones?   Daily Practice

From Here to There

How far is it . . .

NOTE Students find the difference between a number and a multiple of 10.

SMH 78–80

1. From 24 to 80? _____

2. From 13 to 30? _____

3. From 32 to 80? _____

4. From 47 to 70? _____

5. From 48 to 70? _____

6. From 1 to 100? _____

7. From 1 to 90? _____

8. From 2 to 90? _____

9. From 0 to 100? _____

1	2	3	4	5	6	7	8	9	10
11	12	13	14	15	16	17	18	19	20
21	22	23	24	25	26	27	28	29	30
31	32	33	34	35	36	37	38	39	40
41	42	43	44	45	46	47	48	49	50
51	52	53	54	55	56	57	58	59	60
61	62	63	64	65	66	67	68	69	70
71	72	73	74	75	76	77	78	79	80
81	82	83	84	85	86	87	88	89	90
91	92	93	94	95	96	97	98	99	100

Ongoing Review

How many cubes were used to make each shape?

10.

10	11	12	13
Ⓐ	Ⓑ	Ⓒ	Ⓓ

11.

15	16	17	18
Ⓐ	Ⓑ	Ⓒ	Ⓓ

100 Chart

1	2	3	4	5	6	7	8	9	10
11	12	13	14	15	16	17	18	19	20
21	22	23	24	25	26	27	28	29	30
31	32	33	34	35	36	37	38	39	40
41	42	43	44	45	46	47	48	49	50
51	52	53	54	55	56	57	58	59	60
61	62	63	64	65	66	67	68	69	70
71	72	73	74	75	76	77	78	79	80
81	82	83	84	85	86	87	88	89	90
91	92	93	94	95	96	97	98	99	100

Get to 100 Recording Sheet

Record each turn as you play. Only record the numbers rolled, not the total. When you get to 100 on the gameboard, show that your turns add to 100.

Game 1: I played this game with _____.

Game 2: I played this game with _____.

Name _____ Date _____

How Many Tens? How Many Ones? Daily Practice

How Do YOU Get to 100?

Show how you add each number string.

Example:

✓   ✓   ✓   ✓   ✓   ✓   ✓
26 + 5 + 4 + 15 + 33 + 10 + 7

26 + 4 = 30 ✓
5 + 15 = 20 ✓
33 + 7 = 40 ✓ 30 + 20 + 40 + 10 = 100 ✓

1. 15 + 20 + 34 + 16 + 15

2. 10 + 32 + 15 + 28 + 15

3. 8 + 12 + 25 + 25 + 30

4. 42 + 13 + 15 + 8 + 22

Ongoing Review

5. Which combination of 10 describes this cube train?

(A) 3 + 7   (B) 4 + 6   (C) 5 + 5   (D) 9 + 1

Collect $1.00 Recording Sheet

Play *Collect $1.00.* On each turn, write the amount
you collect and the total you have.

	How much did you collect?	How much money do you have now?
Turn 1		
Turn 2		
Turn 3		
Turn 4		
Turn 5		
Turn 6		
Turn 7		
Turn 8		
Turn 9		
Turn 10		
Turn 11		
Turn 12		
Turn 13		
Turn 14		
Turn 15		

Name _____   Date _____

How Many Tens? How Many Ones?   **Daily Practice**

Counting Coins

How much money does each student have?
How much more does each need to make $1.00?

NOTE Students practice counting money and determining the difference between the amount they count and $1.00.

SMH 19, 20, 21

1.

Kira has _____.

Kira needs _____ to make $1.00.

2.

Jake has _____.

Jake needs _____ to make $1.00.

3.

Franco has _____.

Franco needs _____ to make $1.00.

4.

Sally has _____.

Sally needs _____ to make $1.00.

Missing Numbers: Equations (page 1 of 2)

Solve these problems. Fill in the numbers on the 100 chart.

$25 + 10 + 10 =$ _____

$40 + 20 =$ _____

$36 - 10 - 10 =$ _____

$73 + 20 =$ _____

$52 + 10 - 10 + 10 =$ _____

$19 + 10 + 10 + 10 =$ _____

$11 + 10 + 20 =$ _____

$68 - 10 - 10 - 10 =$ _____

$44 + 10 + 20 + 10 =$ _____

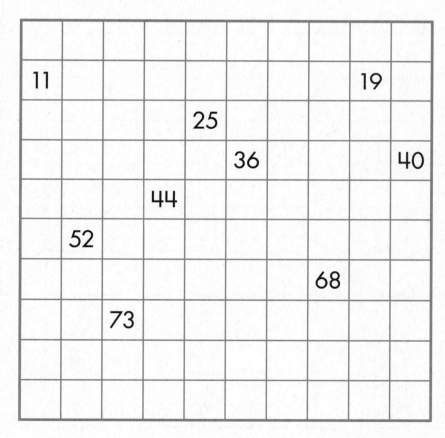

Challenge:

$39 + 10 + 10 + 2 =$ _____

$98 - 20 - 10 - 3 =$ _____

$42 + 10 + 10 + 10 + 5 =$ _____

$71 - 10 - 10 + 20 + 7 =$ _____

Missing Numbers: Equations (page 2 of 2)

$43 + 10 + 10 + 10 =$ _____ $55 + 30 - 20 =$ _____

$35 + 40 =$ _____ $18 + 20 + 10 =$ _____

$33 - 10 - 20 =$ _____ $91 - 10 - 10 - 10 =$ _____

$74 + 10 =$ _____ $22 - 20 + 10 + 10 =$ _____

$67 + 10 - 10 - 10 =$ _____

			5						
							28		
	32								
41									50
		54							
	63								
								89	
				96					

Challenge:

$20 + 20 + 20 + 4 =$ _____ $36 + 10 + 20 + 10 + 3 =$ _____

$87 + 10 - 20 - 6 =$ _____ $51 - 20 - 10 + 8 =$ _____

Missing Numbers: More Equations (page 1 of 2)

Solve these problems. Fill in the numbers on the 100 chart.

25 + 10 + 10 + 5 = _____   49 − 20 − 9 = _____

97 − 20 − 30 − 5 = _____   66 + 10 + 5 = _____

12 + 20 + 8 + 3 = _____   52 − 10 − 6 = _____

45 + 25 + 13 + 17 = _____   100 − 25 − 25 − 15 = _____

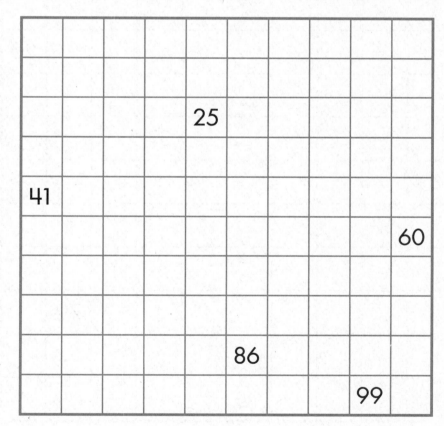

Challenge:

45 + 20 − 15 + 3 = _____   83 − 10 − 10 − 3 = _____

17 + 10 + 10 + 3 = _____   79 − 30 − 10 + 5 + 20 = _____

Missing Numbers:
More Equations (page 2 of 2)

35 + 30 + 5 = _____   23 − 10 + 20 − 3 = _____

78 − 30 − 10 − 5 = _____   46 + 5 + 20 = _____

67 + 20 + 10 − 7 = _____   83 − 20 − 8 = _____

15 + 30 + 5 + 9 = _____   100 − 20 − 20 − 5 − 15 = _____

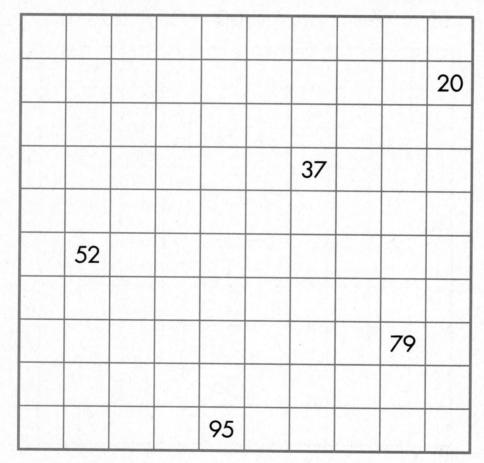

Challenge:

55 + 10 − 25 + 4 = _____   28 + 10 + 15 + 15 + 4 = _____

91 − 10 − 15 − 5 − 8 = _____ 62 − 30 − 20 − 5 + 20 = _____

Do You Have $1.00?

Circle YES or NO.

NOTE Students practice counting money and determine whether the total is $1.00.

SMH 19, 20, 21

You Have These Coins:	Do You Have $1.00?
1.	YES NO
2.	YES NO
3.	YES NO
4.	YES NO
5.	YES NO

Ongoing Review

6. Look at the chart. How many students would rather take a trip to the mountains than to the ocean?

Ⓐ 14   Ⓑ 13   Ⓒ 11   Ⓓ 10

Favorite Trips

Mountains	Ocean
X X X X	X X X X
X X X X	X X X X
X X X X	X X X
X	

48 Unit 6

Did They Get to 100? (page 1 of 2)

NOTE Students show how they would solve a problem with several addends to prove that they equal at least 100.

SMH 54

Sally and Jake were playing *Get to 100*. Add the numbers for each game to see whether they really did get to 100.

Game 1:

20 + 15 + 10 + 10 + 20 + 5 + 10

Did they get to 100? _____

If not, how much more do they need to get to 100? _____

Game 2:

15 + 10 + 15 + 15 + 10 + 5 + 10 + 15 + 5

Did they get to 100? _____

If not, how much more do they need to get to 100? _____

Did They Get to 100? (page 2 of 2)

Game 3:

10 + 15 + 20 + 10 + 20 + 5 + 10 + 5 + 5

Did they get to 100? _____

If not, how much more do they need to get to 100? _____

Game 4:

15 + 10 + 15 + 15 + 10 + 5 + 10 + 5

Did they get to 100? _____

If not, how much more do they need to get to 100? _____

Name _____   Date _____

How Many Tens? How Many Ones?   Daily Practice

Get to 100

Franco, Kira, and Sally are playing *Get to 100*. Below are the numbers they rolled. How much do they have so far? How much more do they need to get to 100? Show your work.

NOTE Students practice adding multiples of 5 and determining how far the totals are from 100.

SMH **54, 78–80**

Kira's Rolls: 20 + 5 + 35 + 20 + 15

Kira's Total: _____

Kira needs _____ to get to 100.

Franco's Rolls: 10 + 5 + 25 + 30 + 5 + 10

Franco's Total: _____

Franco needs _____ to get to 100.

Sally's Rolls: 25 + 25 + 5 + 5 + 25 + 15

Sally's Total: _____

Sally needs _____ to get to 100.

Spend $1.00 Recording Sheet

Play *Spend $1.00*. On each turn, write the amount
you spend and the total you have.

	How much did you spend?	How much money do you have now?
Turn 1		
Turn 2		
Turn 3		
Turn 4		
Turn 5		
Turn 6		
Turn 7		
Turn 8		
Turn 9		
Turn 10		
Turn 11		
Turn 12		
Turn 13		
Turn 14		
Turn 15		

The Dollar Store

NOTE Students practice working with money by determining the difference between an amount and $1.00.

SMH 19, 20, 21

1. How much more money do you need to buy each toy?

You Have This Much:	Cost of Toy	You Need This Much More:
85¢	$1.00	15¢
60¢	$1.00	
30¢	$1.00	
55¢	$1.00	
25¢	$1.00	
90¢	$1.00	
100¢	$1.00	

Ongoing Review

2. Which combination does **not** make 12?

(A) 7 + 5   (B) 8 + 4   (C) 9 + 3   (D) 10 + 1 + 0

How Many Stickers? (page 1 of 2)

Solve each problem. Show your work and write an equation.

NOTE Students solve problems about Sticker Station, a store that sells stickers in strips of 10 and individually as singles. These problems focus on addition, subtraction, and place value (10s and 1s).

SMH 62–64, 70–72

1. Kira bought 6 strips of ten skateboarding stickers and 7 single skateboarding stickers from Sticker Station. She also bought 3 strips of ten butterfly stickers and 3 single butterfly stickers. How many stickers did Kira buy?

2. Jake went to Sticker Station and bought 10 strips of ten train stickers. He gave 4 strips of ten and 2 singles to Sally. How many train stickers does Jake have left?

How Many Stickers? (page 2 of 2)

3. Franco bought 10 strips of ten frog stickers from Sticker Station. He gave 6 strips of ten frog stickers and 6 single frog stickers to Jake. How many frog stickers does Franco have left?

4. Sally went to Sticker Station. She bought 7 strips of ten cloud stickers and 4 single cloud stickers. She also bought 2 strips of ten horse stickers and 3 single horse stickers. How many stickers did Sally buy?

Groups of 10

NOTE Students use what they know about groups of 10s and 1s to solve a story problem.

 39

Mr. T has 83 paper clips. He needs to give each student 10 paper clips for a project they are working on. How many students will get 10 paper clips? Are there any extra paper clips?

Solve the problem. Show your work.

How Many 5s in 100?

1. If you were going to fill in every fifth square on a blank 100 chart, how many numbers would you write? (Hint: These are the numbers you say when you count by 5s.)

How did you figure this out?

2. If you were going to fill in every tenth number on a blank 100 chart, how many numbers would you fill in? (Hint: These are the numbers you say when you count by 10s.)

How did you figure this out?

3. Fill in the count by 5s numbers on a blank 100 chart.

How Many Nickels? (page 1 of 2)

Solve each problem and explain your solution.

1. I have 50 cents in my pocket. I have only nickels in my pocket. How many nickels do I have?

How Many Nickels? (page 2 of 2)

2. a. How many dimes are in 70 cents?

b. How many nickels are in 70 cents?

3. a. How many dimes are in 65 cents?

b. How many nickels are in 65 cents?

Multiples of 5

Write as many equations as you can to make the number in the box. Use only multiples of 5. You can use addition and subtraction.

NOTE Students write equations that equal 75 and 100 using multiples of 5. There are many possible solutions.

 38

1. 75

$$25 + 25 + 25 = 75$$
$$10 + 20 + 30 + 10 + 5 = 75$$

2. 100

Skip-Counting Patterns (page 1 of 2) ✏️WRITING

Use your skip-counting strips to answer
these questions.

1. What do you notice about the numbers when
you count by 2s?

2. What do you notice about the numbers when
you count by 5s?

3. What do you notice about the numbers when
you count by 10s?

Skip-Counting Patterns (page 2 of 2)

Solve each problem. Explain your thinking.

1. Kira counted by 1s to 150. How many numbers
   did she write?

2. Kira counted by 2s to 150. How many numbers
   did she write?

3. Kira counted by 5s to 150. How many numbers
   did she write?

4. Kira counted by 10s to 150. How many numbers
   did she write?

Coin Problems (page 1 of 2)

Solve each problem. Show your work and write an equation.

1. a. How many dimes are in 80 cents?

b. How many nickels are in 80 cents?

2. Kira has 6 dimes and 8 nickels. How much money does Kira have?

Coin Problems (page 2 of 2)

3. Jake spent 35 cents on a pencil and 55 cents on a ball. How much money did Jake spend?

4. Kira has one dollar and 20 cents. She spent 50 cents on a balloon and 20 cents on some stickers. How much money did Kira spend? How much money does she have left?

Skip Counting

Write the missing numbers on the skip-counting strips.

NOTE Students practice counting by 2s, 5s, and 10s.

SMH **37, 38, 39**

2	5	10	34
4	10	20	36
6	15	30	38

Skip-Counting Strips

(page 1 of 2)

Write the missing numbers on the skip-counting strips.

NOTE Students practice counting by 1s, 2s, 5s, and 10s.

SMH **24, 37, 38, 39**

76	8	35	10
77	10	40	20
78	12	45	30

Skip-Counting Strips (page 2 of 2)

83	**20**	**15**	**18**
84	**30**	**20**	**20**
85	**40**	**25**	**22**

Name _____ Date _____

How Many Tens? How Many Ones?   Daily Practice

Missing Number Problems

NOTE Students practice solving addition combinations and sequencing numbers to 150.

SMH 26

1. Solve these problems. Fill in the totals on the chart below.

30 + 50 = _____   20 + 35 = _____   110 + 10 = _____

50 + 10 = _____   50 + 40 = _____   90 + 10 + 20 = _____

65 + 10 = _____   20 + 75 = _____   100 + 20 + 20 = _____

2. Fill in the other missing numbers on the chart.

51	52	53			56	57		59	
61			64	65			68	69	70
	72		74		76	77	78		
81		83	84		86		88	89	
91	92	93			96	97	98	99	100
101	102			105	106				110
111	112	113		115		117	118	119	
121			124			127			130
	132	133			136		138	139	
	142			145	146	147			150

Kids in Business!

Jan, Pat, and Sara make friendship bracelets to sell. Here are the prices.

	Rope bracelet	5¢
	Yarn bracelet	10¢
	Bead bracelet	20¢

Solve each problem and explain your solution.

1. One day, the girls sold 5 rope bracelets, 2 yarn bracelets, and 1 bead bracelet. How much money did they make?

2. Another day, they made 75¢ altogether.

Which bracelets could they have sold?

3. Another day, they made 90¢ altogether.

Which bracelets could they have sold?

Name _____ Date _____

How Many Tens? How Many Ones?　　Daily Practice

Plus or Minus 10

Write the number that is 10 more or 10 less than the target number.

NOTE Students practice adding 10 to and subtracting 10 from a given number.

SMH 26

Minus 10	Target Number	Plus 10
	50	
	76	
	83	
	95	
	100	
	111	
	128	
	132	
	149	
	155	
	176	

How Many Stickers? (page 1 of 2)

Number	Sticker Notation	Sheets, Strips, Singles	Hundreds, Tens, Ones	Equation
135	(sticker notation drawing)	___ Sheets ___ Strips ___ Singles	___ Hundreds ___ Tens ___ Ones	
241		___ Sheets ___ Strips ___ Singles	___ Hundreds ___ Tens ___ Ones	
300		___ Sheets ___ Strips ___ Singles	___ Hundreds ___ Tens ___ Ones	
318		___ Sheets ___ Strips ___ Singles	___ Hundreds ___ Tens ___ Ones	

How Many Tens? How Many Ones?

How Many Stickers? (page 2 of 2)

Number	Sticker Notation	Sheets, Strips, Singles	Hundreds, Tens, Ones	Equation
407		____ Sheets ____ Strips ____ Singles	____ Hundreds ____ Tens ____ Ones	
500		____ Sheets ____ Strips ____ Singles	____ Hundreds ____ Tens ____ Ones	
750		____ Sheets ____ Strips ____ Singles	____ Hundreds ____ Tens ____ Ones	
909		____ Sheets ____ Strips ____ Singles	____ Hundreds ____ Tens ____ Ones	

Name _____ Date _____

How Many Tens? How Many Ones?   Daily Practice

Comparing Stickers

Look at the sets of stickers. Circle the set that has more, and tell how you know.

NOTE Students identify the larger number by comparing the number of hundreds, tens, and ones.

1.

How do you know? _____

2.

How do you know? _____

3.

How do you know? _____

Plus or Minus 10 or 100 Recording Sheet

Choose a number to start with. Roll a +/− 10 or
100 cube. Add or subtract the number you roll.
Record an equation. The answer is your new
start number.

If you roll a number that makes less than zero when
you subtract, roll again.

Start Number	+/− 10 or 100	Equation

How Many Stickers?

Find how many stickers are shown. Write an equation that represents each group.

NOTE Students work with place value as they determine a total amount based on the number of hundreds, tens, and ones, and as they represent an amount using place value notation.

Sticker Notation	Equation

Use sticker notation.

Show 246 stickers.	Show 413 stickers.

Hundreds, Tens, and Ones

NOTE Students practice expressing numbers as the sum of hundreds, tens, and ones.

Write an equation that shows the number of tens and ones. Example: 53 = <u>50</u> + <u>3</u>

1. 71 = ____ + ____   **2.** 49 = ____ + ____

3. 36 = ____ + ____   **4.** 50 = ____ + ____

Write an equation that shows the number of hundreds, tens, and ones. Example: 127 = <u>100</u> + <u>20</u> + <u>7</u>

5. 162 = ____ + ____ + ____   **6.** 328 = ____ + ____ + ____

7. 209 = ____ + ____ + ____   **8.** 555 = ____ + ____ + ____

9. 817 = ____ + ____ + ____ **10.** 934 = ____ + ____ + ____

Solve each equation. Example: 80 + 6 = <u>86</u>

11. 40 + 0 = _____   **12.** 90 + 8 = _____

13. 100 + 40 + 5 = _____   **14.** 100 + 4 = _____

15. 200 + 10 + 0 = _____   **16.** 300 + 90 + 7 = _____

Find the Number

Write each number.

1. Start number: 189

10 less	10 more	100 less	100 more

2. Start number: 339

10 less	10 more	100 less	100 more

3. Start number: 571

10 less	10 more	100 less	100 more

4. Start number: 690

10 less	10 more	100 less	100 more

5. Start number: 901

10 less	10 more	100 less	100 more

Name _____   Date _____

How Many Tens? How Many Ones?   Daily Practice

Greater Than/Less Than

Circle the greater number in each pair of numbers. Write the correct symbol in the box between each pair.

NOTE Students compare two numbers and determine which is greater. They record this comparison using <, >, = · notation.

SMH 81

>	<	=
greater than	**less than**	**equal to**

1. 125 ☐ 226   **2.** 386 ☐ 336

3. 789 ☐ 789   **4.** 901 ☐ 890

5. 772 ☐ 776   **6.** 302 ☐ 299

Name _____   Date _____

How Many Tens? How Many Ones?   Daily Practice

How Many Stickers?

James bought the following amounts of stickers at Sticker Station. Find the total amount of stickers James bought.

NOTE Students combine four numbers to determine the total amount of stickers.

SMH **32**

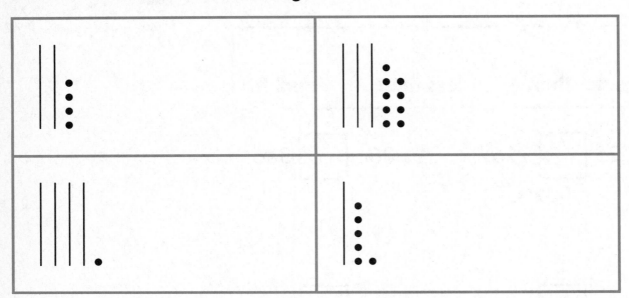

Write an equation and show how you figured this out.

How many stickers did James buy in all? _____

Complicated Kris Northern

"This image illustrates some of the best qualities of fractals—infinity, reiteration, and self similarity."– **Kris Northern**

Investigations
IN NUMBER, DATA, AND SPACE®

Parts of a Whole, Parts of a Group

Parts of a Whole, Parts of a Group

Linda and Ebony Share Everything (page 1 of 5)

Linda and Ebony are twins who share everything equally.

1. Their mother gave Linda and Ebony a sandwich.

Draw a line to show how much Linda got and how much Ebony got.

Color Linda's half red. Color Ebony's half blue.

2. Their mother brought Linda and Ebony a strip of stickers.

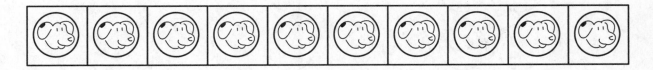

Color Linda's half red. Color Ebony's half blue.

How many stickers did Linda get? _____

How many stickers did Ebony get? _____

Linda and Ebony Share Everything (page 2 of 5)

3. Their grandmother gave Linda and Ebony a heart filled with treats.

Draw a line to show how much Linda got and how much Ebony got.

Color Linda's half red. Color Ebony's half blue.

4. Their older brother gave them 18 marbles.

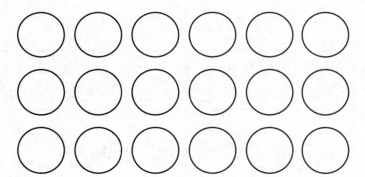

Color Linda's half red. Color Ebony's half blue.

How many marbles did Linda get? _____

How many marbles did Ebony get? _____

Linda and Ebony Share Everything (page 3 of 5)

5. Their brother brought them a ball of clay.

Draw a line to show how much Linda got and how much Ebony got.

Color Linda's half red. Color Ebony's half blue.

6. Their friend gave Linda and Ebony 28 blocks.

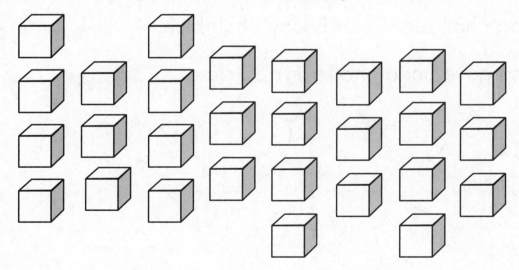

Color Linda's half red. Color Ebony's half blue.

How many blocks did Linda get? _____

How many blocks did Ebony get? _____

Linda and Ebony Share Everything (page 4 of 5)

7. Their grandfather brought them a hexagon filled with treats.

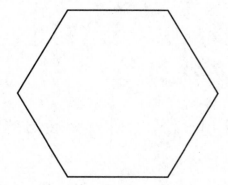

Draw a line to show how much Linda got and how much Ebony got.

Color Linda's half red. Color Ebony's half blue.

8. Their friend gave Linda and Ebony 32 stars.

Color Linda's half red. Color Ebony's half blue.

How many stars did Linda get? _____

How many stars did Ebony get? _____

Linda and Ebony
Share Everything (page 5 of 5)

9. Their uncle brought them a triangle filled with treats.

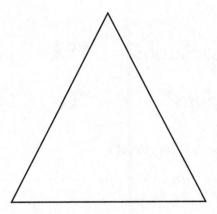

Draw a line to show how much Linda got and how much Ebony got.

Color Linda's half red. Color Ebony's half blue.

10. Their aunt gave Linda and Ebony 40 happy faces.

Color Linda's half red. Color Ebony's half blue.

How many happy faces did Linda get? _____

How many happy faces did Ebony get? _____

How Many?

There are 22 students in Mr. G's class.
He has 48 balloons.

Mr. G wants to give 2 balloons to
each student.

> **NOTE** Students use what they know about groups of 2 to solve a story problem.

1. Will each student get 2 balloons?   YES   NO

2. Are there any extra balloons?   YES   NO

3. Solve the problem. Show your work.

Build the Geoblock (page 1 of 2)

1. Put Geoblocks together to build this block.

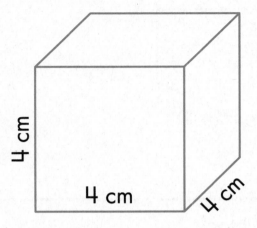

Is each part half? _____

2. Put Geoblocks together to build this block.

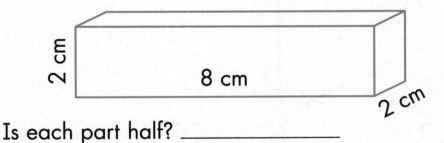

Is each part half? _____

3. Put Geoblocks together to build this block.

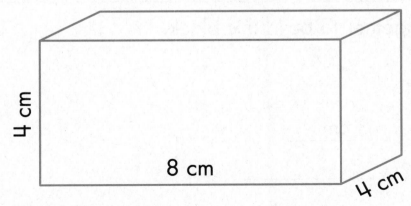

Is each part half? _____

Build the Geoblock (page 2 of 2)

4. Put Geoblocks together to build this block.

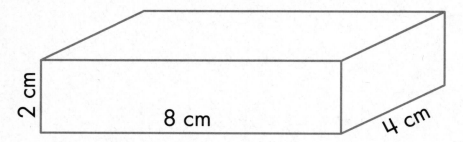

2 cm

8 cm

4 cm

Is each part half? _____

---

5. Put Geoblocks together to build this block.

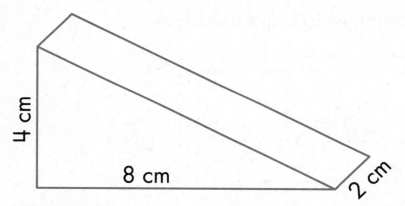

4 cm

8 cm

2 cm

Is each part half? _____

---

6. Put Geoblocks together to build this block.

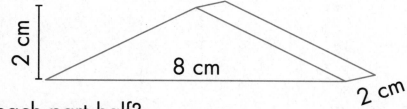

2 cm

8 cm

2 cm

Is each part half? _____

Bunches of Balloons (page 1 of 2)

On Saturday, Linda and Ebony will have a birthday. Some of their friends and relatives send them birthday balloons early.

1. On Monday, 7 balloons come.

   Can each girl get $\frac{1}{2}$ of the balloons? _____

   How many does Linda get? _____

   How many does Ebony get? _____

2. On Tuesday, 8 balloons come.

   Can each girl get $\frac{1}{2}$ of the balloons? _____

   How many does Linda get? _____

   How many does Ebony get? _____

3. On Wednesday, 14 balloons come.

   Can each girl get $\frac{1}{2}$ of the balloons? _____

   How many does Linda get? _____

   How many does Ebony get? _____

Bunches of Balloons (page 2 of 2)

4. On Thursday, 11 balloons come.

Can each girl get $\frac{1}{2}$ of the balloons? _____

How many does Linda get? _____

How many does Ebony get? _____

5. On Friday, 20 balloons come.

Can each girl get $\frac{1}{2}$ of the balloons? _____

How many does Linda get? _____

How many does Ebony get? _____

6. On Saturday they say, "It's hard to keep track of whose balloons are whose!" So they put all of their balloons together and add them up.

How many balloons came that week? _____

Can each girl get $\frac{1}{2}$ of the balloons? _____

How many does Linda get? _____

How many does Ebony get? _____

Sharing Pennies (page 1 of 2)

Linda and Ebony place all of the pennies they save in a jar. Sometimes they empty the jar, count out the pennies, and figure out how to share them equally. Then they put the pennies back.

1. On Monday, the girls counted 14 pennies in their jar.

Can each girl get $\frac{1}{2}$ of the pennies? _____

How many does Linda get? _____

How many does Ebony get? _____

2. On Tuesday, they found 7 more pennies and added them to the jar. They counted all the pennies in the jar.

Can each girl get $\frac{1}{2}$ of the pennies? _____

How many does Linda get? _____

How many does Ebony get? _____

3. On Wednesday, their sister gave them 9 pennies. They put them in the jar.

Can each girl get $\frac{1}{2}$ of the pennies? _____

How many does Linda get? _____

How many does Ebony get? _____

Sharing Pennies (page 2 of 2)

4. On Thursday, their mother added 6 pennies to their jar.

Can each girl get $\frac{1}{2}$ of the pennies? _____

How many does Linda get? _____

How many does Ebony get? _____

5. On Friday, their father put 18 pennies in their jar.

Can each girl get $\frac{1}{2}$ of the pennies? _____

How many does Linda get? _____

How many does Ebony get? _____

6. On Saturday, they counted up all of their pennies.

How many pennies do they have? _____

Show your work.

Halves and Not Halves

Color the shape if the line shows halves.

NOTE Students determine which shapes are divided into halves by the given line.

SMH **84, 86**

1.

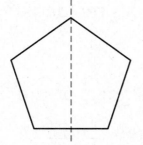

2.

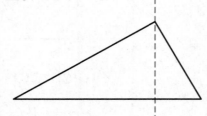

3.

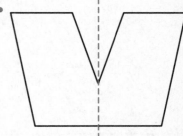

4.

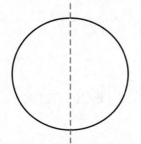

5.

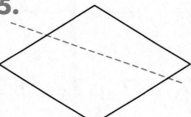

6.

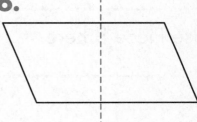

7.

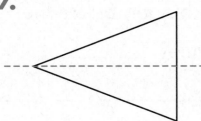

8.

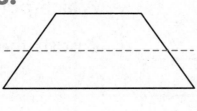

9.

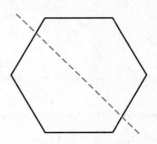

Ongoing Review

10. Which equation describes the groups of dots?

(A) $5 + 5 = 10$ (C) $5 + 6 = 11$

(B) $2 + 5 = 7$ (D) $4 + 4 = 8$

Halves and Not Halves of Rectangles (page 1 of 2)

Use Piece A here.

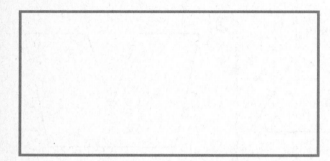

Is Piece A $\frac{1}{2}$ of this rectangle?

_____

Which part is bigger, or are the 2 parts the same? _____

Use Piece B here.

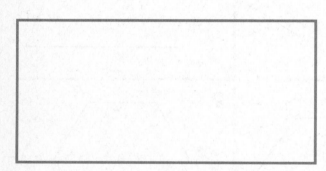

Is Piece B $\frac{1}{2}$ of this rectangle?

_____

Which part is bigger, or are the 2 parts the same? _____

Use Piece C here.

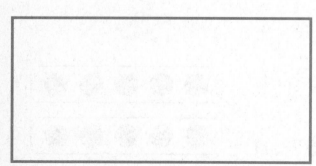

Is Piece C $\frac{1}{2}$ of this rectangle?

_____

Which part is bigger, or are the 2 parts the same? _____

Halves and Not Halves
of Rectangles (page 2 of 2)

Use Piece D here.

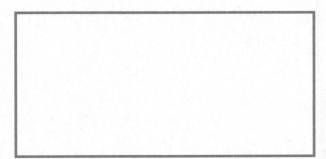

Is Piece D $\frac{1}{2}$ of this rectangle?

_____

Which part is bigger, or are the

2 parts the same? _____

Use Piece E here.

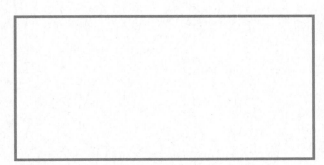

Is Piece E $\frac{1}{2}$ of this rectangle?

_____

Which part is bigger, or are the

2 parts the same? _____

Use Piece F here.

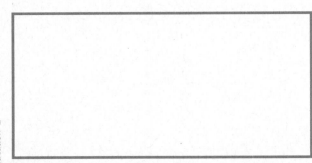

Is Piece F $\frac{1}{2}$ of this rectangle?

_____

Which part is bigger, or are the

2 parts the same? _____

Sticker Station

NOTE Students use what they know about groups of 10s and 1s to solve a story problem.

 62–64

Franco went to Sticker Station.

He bought 4 strips of 10s and 7 singles of fish stickers.

Then he bought 3 strips of 10s and 3 singles of boat stickers.

How many stickers did Franco buy?

Solve the problem. Show your work.
Write an equation.

Going on a Picnic (page 1 of 2)

Linda and Ebony are going on a picnic, so their mother packed a lunch for them.

1. They have 3 sandwiches. They share the sandwiches evenly. How many sandwiches does each girl get?

2. They have 5 pieces of cheese. They share the cheese evenly. How many pieces of cheese does each girl get?

3. They have 9 strawberries. They share the strawberries evenly. How many strawberries does each girl get?

4. They have 11 carrot sticks. They share the carrot sticks evenly. How many carrot sticks does each girl get?

5. They have 7 celery sticks. They share the celery sticks evenly. How many celery sticks does each girl get?

Going on a Picnic (page 2 of 2)

6. Linda and Ebony have 15 peanuts. They share the peanuts evenly. How many peanuts does each girl get?

7. They have 21 crackers. They share the crackers evenly. How many crackers does each girl get?

8. They have 27 blackberries. They share the blackberries evenly. How many blackberries does each girl get?

9. For dessert they share a bag of raisins. There are 39 raisins. They share the raisins evenly. How many raisins does each girl get?

Buying Stickers

Sally and Franco are buying stickers at Sticker Station.

NOTE Students use their understanding of coins and counting by 5s and 10s to solve problems about money.

SMH **19, 38, 39**

1. Franco's stickers cost 75¢.

He has only nickels in his pocket.

How many nickels does he need to buy his stickers?

Solve the problem. Show your work.

2. Sally's stickers cost 80¢.
She has 9 dimes in her pocket.
Does Sally have enough dimes to buy her stickers?   Yes   No

How do you know?

How Many Halves?

Draw one straight line to divide each shape into halves that are the same size and shape.

> **NOTE** Students have been finding one half of objects and sets. Some of these shapes can be divided into congruent halves in more than one way.
>
> **SMH** 84, 86

1.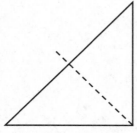

2.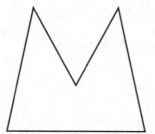

3.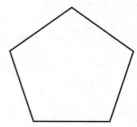

4.

5.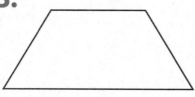

6.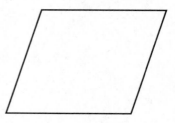

7.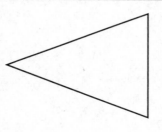

8.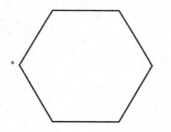

9.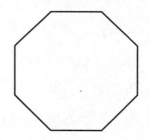

Ongoing Review

10. What number comes next?

1, 3, 5, 7, 9, _____

    9   10   11   12

    Ⓐ   Ⓑ   Ⓒ   Ⓓ

Halves of Groups

Solve each problem. Show your work.

NOTE Students use what they have been learning about fractions to divide groups of people and sets of objects into halves.

SMH 86

1. There are 20 students at the park. One half of them are boys. How many boys are at the park?

2. Kira had 24 flowers. She gave half of them to her mother. How many flowers did Kira give to her mother? How many flowers does she have left?

3. Twelve friends went to the movies. One half of them sat in the front row, and the other half sat in the middle row. How many friends sat in the front row?

4. Franco had $30.00. He spent half of his money on a new football. How much money did he spend?

Fraction Flags (page 1 of 4)

Color each part of the flag a different color. Then write what fraction of the flag each color is.

Flag 1

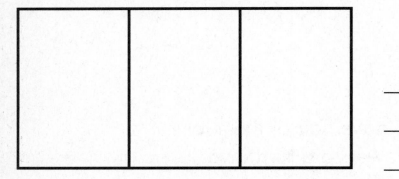

_____

_____

_____

Flag 2

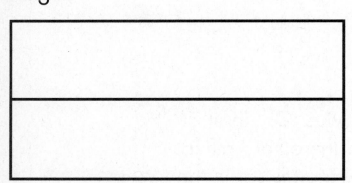

_____

_____

Flag 3

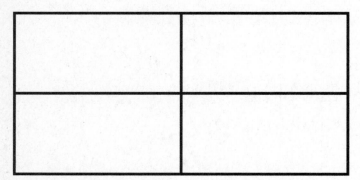

_____

_____

_____

_____

Fraction Flags (page 2 of 4)

Color each part of the flag a different color. Then write what fraction of the flag each color is.

Flag 4

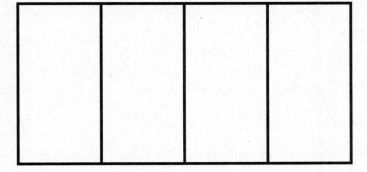

_____

_____

_____

_____

Flag 5

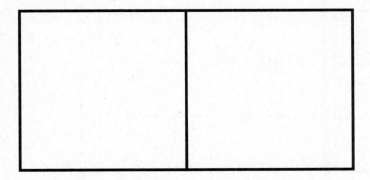

_____

_____

Flag 6

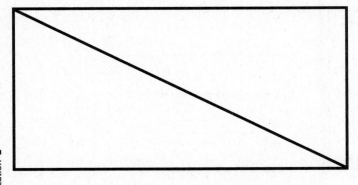

_____

_____

Fraction Flags (page 3 of 4)

Color each part of the flag a different color. Then write what fraction of the flag each color is.

Flag 7

_____

_____

_____

Flag 8

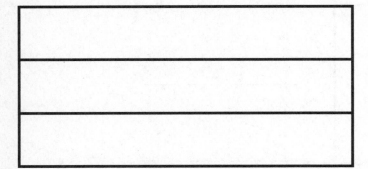

_____

_____

_____

Flag 9

_____

_____

_____

_____

Fraction Flags (page 4 of 4)

Color each part of the flag a different color. Then write what fraction of the flag each color is.

Flag 10

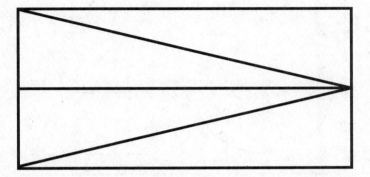

_____

_____

_____

_____

Flag 11

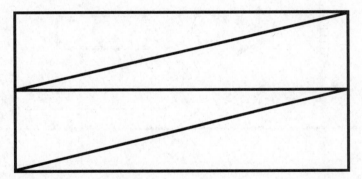

_____

_____

_____

_____

Flag 12

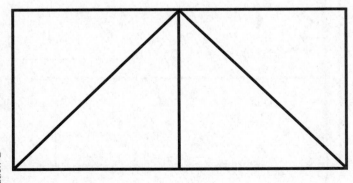

_____

_____

_____

_____

What Time Is It?

Read each clock, and write the digital time
and the time in words.

NOTE *Students practice
telling time to the hour, the
half hour, and the quarter
hour.*

SMH 137–138, 139, 140

Example:

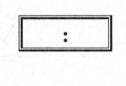

1 : 30

one-thirty

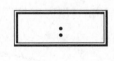

:

_____

:

_____

:

_____

:

_____

:

_____

:

_____

:

_____

Circles: Half-and-Half

1. Draw a line that cuts the circle in half.

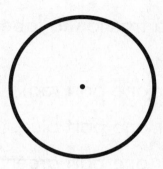

2. Color half of the circle.

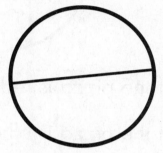

3. Look at the circles.

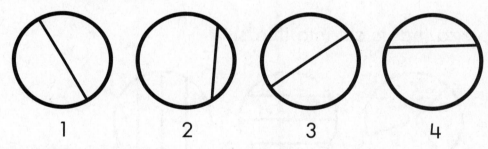

    1   2   3   4

a. Which circles are cut in half? _____

b. Which circles are **not** cut in half? _____

c. Explain how you know which circles are cut in half and which are not cut in half.

_____

_____

_____

Pizza Fractions

NOTE Students use what they know about fractions to answer questions.

1. Use a fraction to label each part of the pizza.

Color one part red.

Color one part blue.

Color one part green.

a. What fraction of the pizza is red?_____

b. What fraction of the pizza is blue? _____

c. What fraction of the pizza is green? _____

2. Circle the pizza that is cut into thirds.

   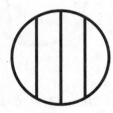

Explain why you think this pizza is cut into thirds.

_____

_____

_____

_____

Different Shapes: Fourths

NOTE Students divide shapes into equal parts.

1. Find three different ways to divide these squares into fourths.

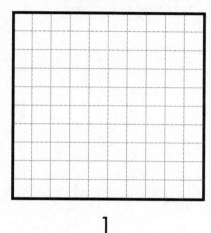   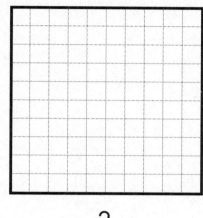   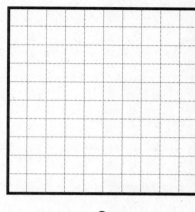

1   2   3

2. In Square 1, color $\frac{2}{4}$ blue and $\frac{1}{4}$ red.

What fraction of the square is colored? _____

What fraction of the square is **not** colored? _____

3. In Square 2, color $\frac{1}{2}$ green and $\frac{1}{4}$ blue.

How many fourths are green? _____

4. In Square 3, color $\frac{1}{4}$ red and $\frac{3}{4}$ green.

What fraction of the square is colored? _____

More Fractions (page 1 of 4)

Color each part of the flag a different color. Then write what fraction of the flag each color is.

1.

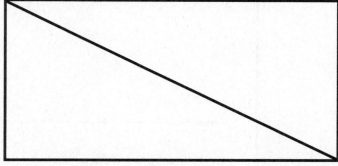

_____

_____

2.

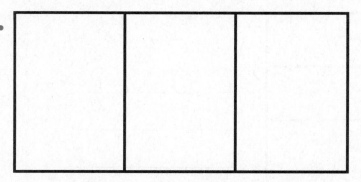

_____

_____

3.

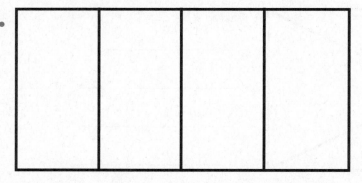

_____

_____

_____

4.

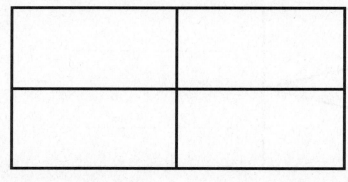

_____

_____

_____

_____

More Fractions (page 2 of 4)

Color each part of the flag a different color. Then write what fraction of the flag each color is.

5.

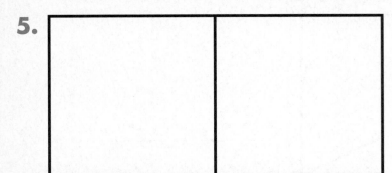

_____

_____

6.

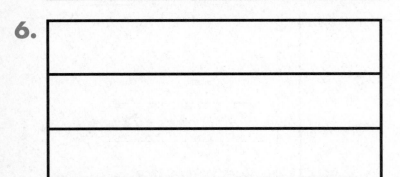

_____

_____

_____

7.

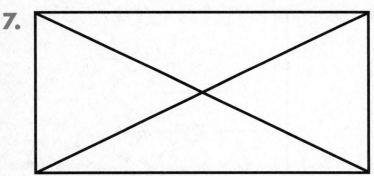

_____

_____

_____

_____

8.

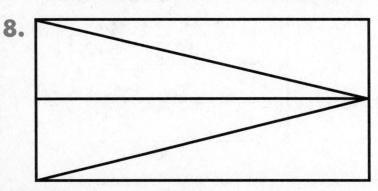

_____

_____

_____

_____

More Fractions (page 3 of 4)

Color each part of the flag a different color. Then write what fraction of the flag each color is.

9.

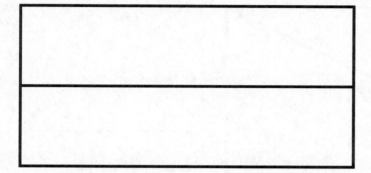

_____

_____

10.

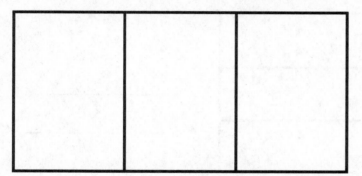

_____

_____

11.

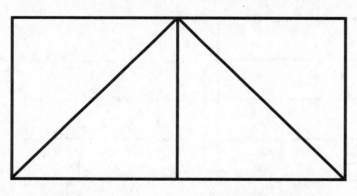

_____

_____

_____

12.

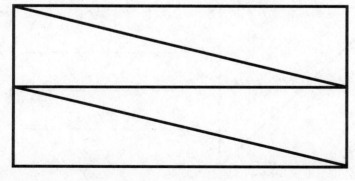

_____

_____

_____

More Fractions (page 4 of 4)

Color each part of the flag a different color. Then write what fraction of the flag each color is.

13.

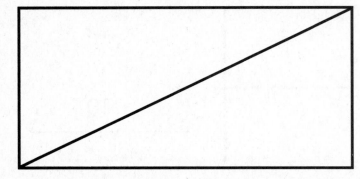

_____

_____

14.

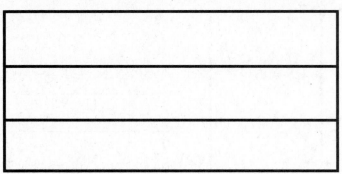

_____

_____

_____

15.

_____

_____

_____

_____

16.

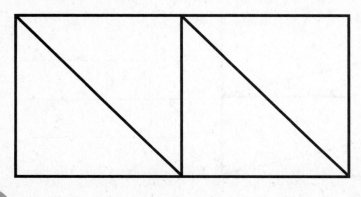

_____

_____

_____

Today's Number

Circle all of the problems that equal
Today's Number.

NOTE Students determine
which expressions are
equal to "Today's Number."

SMH 55, 56

Today's Number is 20.

7 + 3 + 6 + 4	31 − 10
4 + 2 + 4 + 4 + 3 + 1	41 − 19
37 − 17	15 + 2 + 6
46 − 26	14 + 3 + 3
10 + 9 + 1	7 + 8 + 9 + 1

Color Them In!

In each box, show 2 ways to draw fourths. Color each fourth a different color.

NOTE Students use 3 or 4 colors to illustrate thirds and fourths of rectangles in 2 ways.

 84, 87, 90

1.

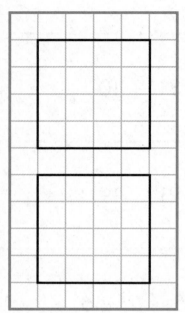

2.

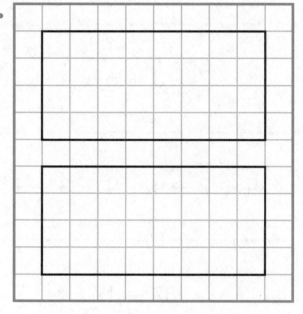

Show 2 ways to draw thirds. Color each third a different color.

3.

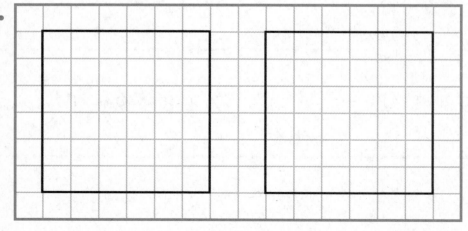

Friends at Play (page 1 of 2)

Linda, Ebony, and Kira are playing together.

1. Kira's mother gave them 24 peanuts. Each girl gets one third of the peanuts.

How many peanuts does each girl get? _____

How did you figure it out?

2. The girls have 15 stickers. Each girl gets one third of the stickers.

How many stickers does each girl get? _____

How did you figure it out?

3. The girls play a game with 30 cards. Each girl gets one third of the cards.

How many cards does each girl get? _____

How did you figure it out?

Friends at Play (page 2 of 2)

Jake, Bob, Tim, and David are playing together.

4. Jake's mother gave them 32 peanuts. Each boy
gets one fourth of the peanuts.
How many peanuts does each boy get? _____

How did you figure it out?

5. The boys have 24 stickers. Each boy gets
one fourth of the stickers.
How many stickers does each boy get? _____

How did you figure it out?

6. The boys are playing a game with 28 cards.
Each boy gets one fourth of the cards.
How many cards does each boy get? _____

How did you figure it out?

Sharing Lunch

Solve each problem. Show your work.

1. Jake, Bob, Tim, and David are having lunch together. Jake's mother puts out 6 carrot sticks for them to share. Each boy gets one fourth of 6 carrot sticks. How many carrot sticks does each boy get? _____

   How did you figure it out?

2. Jake's mother puts out 7 sandwiches for the boys to share. Each boy gets one fourth of 7 sandwiches. How many sandwiches does each boy get? _____

   How did you figure it out?

3. Jake's mother puts out 9 slices of apple for the boys to share. Each boy gets one fourth of 9 slices. How many slices does each boy get? _____

   How did you figure it out?

Halves, Thirds, and Fourths of Groups

Solve each problem. Show your work.

NOTE Students use what they have been learning about fractions to divide groups of people and sets of objects into halves, thirds, and fourths.

SMH 86, 87, 90

1. There are 28 students in the class.
One half of the students are girls.
How many of the students are girls?

2. Sally had $12.00. She used one fourth of her money to buy lunch. How much money did her lunch cost?

3. Jake has 9 shells. He gives one third of his shells to Franco. How many shells did Jake give to Franco? How many shells does Jake have left?

4. There are 26 people in the store. One half of them are children. How many children are in the store?

Fractions All Around Us

NOTE Students identify fractions in real-life objects.

SMH **84, 86, 87, 90, 92**

1. Justin makes a grilled cheese sandwich. His three brothers want to try it. Draw lines to show how Justin cuts the sandwich so that he can share it evenly with all his brothers.

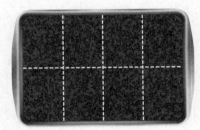

2. Auntie Courtney cut a cake.

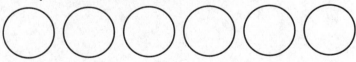

Is the cake cut into thirds, fourths, or eighths?

3. Jeff's class orders 6 pizzas for lunch. After they are done, there are $2\frac{3}{4}$ pizzas left over. Color in the pizza that is left over.

◯ ◯ ◯ ◯ ◯ ◯

4. What fraction of the pizza did the class eat? Explain how you know.

Complicated Kris Northern

"This image illustrates some of the best qualities of fractals—infinity, reiteration, and self similarity."– **Kris Northern**

Investigations
IN NUMBER, DATA, AND SPACE®

Student Activity Book

Partners, Teams, and Paper Clips

UNIT 8

Partners, Teams, and Paper Clips

Investigation 4

Investigation 5A

Problems About Two Groups (page 1 of 2)

Solve the problems. Show your work.

1. 12 children from Room A want to play kickball.
   10 children from Room B also want
   to play. Can they make 2 equal teams?

   How many people would be on each team? _____

2. Ms. Todd's class is going to play a game in
   pairs. There are 12 boys and 10 girls. Can
   everyone have a partner?

   How many pairs would there be? _____

3. There are 12 girls and 11 boys in Mr. Fox's class.
   Can everyone have a partner?

   How many pairs would there be? _____

Problems About Two Groups (page 2 of 2)

Solve the problems. Show your work.

4. 16 children from Room A want to play soccer.
11 children from Room B also want to play.
Can they make 2 equal teams?

How many people would be on each team? _____

5. At recess 17 girls want to play baseball. 13 boys
want to play, too. Can they make 2 equal teams?

How many people would be on each team? _____

6. Ms. Ortega's class has 15 girls and 15 boys.
Can everyone have a partner?

How many pairs would there be? _____

At the Amusement Park

Solve each problem. Show your work.

NOTE Students determine which numbers can and cannot make equal groups of 2 or 2 equal teams.

SMH 41–42

1. 6 girls and 7 boys want to ride the Python roller coaster together. Can everyone have a partner to ride with?

How many pairs would there be? _____

2. Two groups can go into the Haunted House at one time. There are 26 children in line. Can they make two equal groups?

How many people would be in each group? _____

Ongoing Review

3. David has 13 pets. Some of them are mice, and some of them are hamsters. How many of David's 13 pets could be mice?

Which answer could **not** be correct?

(A) 12   (B) 11   (C) 1   (D) 0

Missing Numbers

Write the missing numbers
on the counting strips.

NOTE Students practice skip counting
by groups of 2s, 5s, and 10s.

SMH 37, 38, 39

112		**160**
114		
	125	**140**
		130
122	**140**	
124	**145**	
		90

Partners and Teams (page 1 of 2)

Solve each problem. Show your work.

NOTE Students think about numbers that can and cannot make groups of 2 or 2 equal teams.

SMH 41–42

1. Mrs. Abel's class has 10 boys and 9 girls. Can everyone have a partner?

   How many pairs would there be? _____

2. 11 girls want to play kickball. 7 boys also want to play. Can they make 2 equal teams?

   How many people would be on each team? _____

Partners and Teams (page 2 of 2)

Solve each problem. Show your work.

3. Mr. Yoshi has 9 girls and 7 boys in his class.
Can everyone have a partner?

How many pairs would there be? _____

4. There are 8 boys and 11 girls who want to play
soccer. Can they make 2 equal teams?

How many people would be on each team? _____

Can You Make . . . ? (page 1 of 2)

Today's Number is <u>24</u>.

1. Is 24 even or odd? _____

2. Can you make 24 with two EVEN numbers?

_____ + _____ = 24   _____ + _____ = 24

If you think you cannot, explain why:

_____

_____

3. Can you make 24 with two ODD numbers?

_____ + _____ = 24   _____ + _____ = 24

If you think you cannot, explain why:

_____

_____

4. Can you make 24 with an EVEN and an ODD number?

_____ + _____ = 24   _____ + _____ = 24

If you think you cannot, explain why:

_____

_____

Can You Make . . . ? (page 2 of 2)

Today's Number is <u>23</u>.

5. Is 23 even or odd? _____

6. Can you make 23 with two EVEN numbers?

_____ + _____ = 23   _____ + _____ = 23

If you think you cannot, explain why:

_____

_____

7. Can you make 23 with two ODD numbers?

_____ + _____ = 23   _____ + _____ = 23

If you think you cannot, explain why:

_____

_____

8. Can you make 23 with an EVEN and an ODD number?

_____ + _____ = 23   _____ + _____ = 23

If you think you cannot, explain why:

_____

_____

What Happens When . . . ? (page 1 of 3)

What happens when you add
two ODD numbers together?

1. Try these:

9 + 9 = _____   Is the answer even or odd? _____

11 + 7 = _____   Is the answer even or odd? _____

15 + 23 = _____   Is the answer even or odd? _____

2. Now try some of your own:

_____ + _____ = _____   Is the answer even or odd? _____

_____ + _____ = _____   Is the answer even or odd? _____

_____ + _____ = _____   Is the answer even or odd? _____

3. What do you get when you add two ODD numbers together?

_____

4. Do you think this is **always** true? _____

5. Why do you think so? _____

_____

_____

What Happens When . . . ? (page 2 of 3)

What happens when you add
two EVEN numbers together?

6. Try these:

8 + 8 = _____   Is the answer even or odd? _____

12 + 6 = _____   Is the answer even or odd? _____

14 + 20 = _____   Is the answer even or odd? _____

7. Now try some of your own:

_____ + _____ = _____ Is the answer even or odd? _____

_____ + _____ = _____ Is the answer even or odd? _____

_____ + _____ = _____ Is the answer even or odd? _____

8. What do you get when you add two EVEN numbers together?

_____

9. Do you think this is **always** true? _____

10. Why do you think so? _____

_____

_____

What Happens When . . . ? (page 3 of 3)

What happens when you add an EVEN
number and an ODD number?

11. Try these:

8 + 7 = _____   Is the answer even or odd? _____

11 + 6 = _____   Is the answer even or odd? _____

14 + 23 = _____   Is the answer even or odd? _____

12. Now try some of your own:

_____ + _____ = _____ Is the answer even or odd? _____

_____ + _____ = _____ Is the answer even or odd? _____

_____ + _____ = _____ Is the answer even or odd? _____

13. What do you get when you add an EVEN
number and an ODD number?

_____

14. Do you think this is **always** true? _____

15. Why do you think so? _____

_____

_____

Telling Time

Read each clock. Record what time it is. Record and draw what time it will be in 1 hour. Write the time in words.

NOTE Students practice telling, recording, and determining what time it will be to the quarter hour.

SMH 137–138, 140, 141

What time is it now?		What time will it be in one hour?	
	: nine fifteen		: ________
	: ________		: ________
	: ________		: ________
	: ________		: ________
	: ________		: ________

Adding Even and Odd Numbers (page 1 of 2)

NOTE Students investigate what happens when you add two even numbers or two odd numbers.

SMH 41–42

Solve each problem. Circle EVEN or ODD for each answer.

1. $6 + 8 =$ _____   EVEN   ODD

2. $12 + 4 =$ _____   EVEN   ODD

3. $16 + 20 =$ _____   EVEN   ODD

Answer each question. Explain your thinking.

4. What happens when you add two even numbers?

_____

_____

_____

5. Is this true for **any** two even numbers?

6. Explain (or show) **why** this is true.

Adding Even and
Odd Numbers (page 2 of 2) ✏️WRITING

Solve each problem. Circle EVEN or ODD for
each answer.

7. $7 + 9 =$ _____   EVEN   ODD

8. $13 + 5 =$ _____   EVEN   ODD

9. $15 + 21 =$ _____   EVEN   ODD

Answer each question. Explain your thinking.

10. What happens when you add two odd numbers?

_____

_____

_____

11. Is this true for **any** two odd numbers?

12. Explain (or show) **why** this is true.

Even or Odd?

Will the sum be even or odd?
Circle one word.
Solve the problem to check
your answer.

NOTE Students use what they know about adding even and odd numbers to determine whether sums will be even or odd. They also practice addition combinations.

SMH 41–42

	Will the sum be even or odd?	What is the sum?
1. 2 + 4	EVEN ODD	
2. 6 + 3	EVEN ODD	
3. 8 + 7	EVEN ODD	
4. 9 + 2	EVEN ODD	
5. 6 + 6	EVEN ODD	

Ongoing Review

6. How many boats are there?

Ⓐ 19
Ⓑ 20
Ⓒ 21
Ⓓ 22

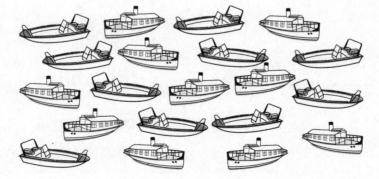

How Much Money?

How much money does each student have? How much more does each one need to make $1.00?

> **NOTE** Students practice counting money and determining the difference between an amount and $1.00.
>
> **SMH** 19, 20, 21

1.

Kira has _____.

She needs _____ to make $1.00.

2.

Franco has _____.

He needs _____ to make $1.00.

3.

Jake has _____.

He needs _____ to make $1.00.

4.

Sally has _____.

She needs _____ to make $1.00.

Plus 9 or 10
BINGO Gameboard

NOTE This game offers practice with plus 9 and plus 10 addition combinations.

SMH 51, 52, G11

9	**10**	**11**	**12**	**13**	**14**
15	**16**	**17**	**18**	**19**	**20**
20	**19**	**18**	**17**	**16**	**15**
14	**13**	**12**	**11**	**10**	**9**
9	**10**	**11**	**12**	**13**	**14**
15	**16**	**17**	**18**	**19**	**20**

Subtracting Tens

Solve these problems. Fill in the answers on the 100 chart below.

> **NOTE** Students practice subtracting 10 and multiples of 10 and sequencing numbers 1–100.
>
> **SMH** 24

1. 43 – 10 = ____   **2.** 54 – 20 = ____   **3.** 95 – 50 = ____

4. 37 – 20 = ____   **5.** 67 – 30 = ____   **6.** 49 – 20 = ____

7. 22 – 10 = ____   **8.** 86 – 30 = ____   **9.** 64 – 40 = ____

10. Fill in the other missing numbers on the 100 chart.

		3			6				10
				15				19	
21				25	26				
		33			36		38		
	42		44					49	50
	52			55		57			
			64				68		
71				75		77			80
		83			86			89	
91					96				

The Remaining Combinations (page 1 of 2)

Choose 3 pairs of problems that are hard for you to remember.

> **NOTE** Students are finding ways to remember facts that are hard for them. Ask your child to explain how the clues help.
>
> **SMH** 53

3 + 5 5 + 3	4 + 7 7 + 4	3 + 8 8 + 3	5 + 8 8 + 5
3 + 6 6 + 3	5 + 7 7 + 5	4 + 8 8 + 4	6 + 8 8 + 6

1. _____ is hard for me to remember.

Here is a clue that can help me:

2. _____ is hard for me to remember.

Here is a clue that can help me:

3. _____ is hard for me to remember.

Here is a clue that can help me:

The Remaining Combinations (page 2 of 2)

Now solve these combinations.

4. $3 + 5 =$ _____

5. $7 + 4 =$ _____

6. $6 + 8 =$ _____

7. $8 + 3 =$ _____

8. $3 + 6 =$ _____

9. $8 + 5 =$ _____

10. $7 + 5 =$ _____

11. $8 + 6 =$ _____

12. $5 + 8 =$ _____

13. $6 + 3 =$ _____

14. $5 + 3 =$ _____

15. $8 + 4 =$ _____

16. $5 + 7 =$ _____

17. $4 + 7 =$ _____

18. $3 + 8 =$ _____

19. $4 + 8 =$ _____

Pennies and Paper Clips (page 1 of 2)

Write an equation. Solve the problem.
Show your work.

1. Franco had 100 pennies. He used 67 of them to buy a baseball card. How many pennies does he have left?

2. There were 100 paper clips in the box. Kira pinched 52 of them. How many paper clips are left in the box?

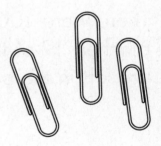

Pennies and Paper Clips (page 2 of 2)

Write an equation. Solve the problem.
Show your work.

3. Sally had 100 pennies. She gave 26 of them to her brother. How many pennies does Sally have now?

4. There were 100 paper clips in the box. Jake pinched 19 of them. How many paper clips are left in the box?

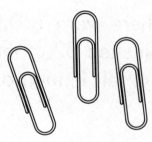

How Many Stickers?

Write an equation. Solve the problem.
Show your work.

NOTE Students solve
a story problem.

SMH **70, 71–72**

1. Sally had 40 airplane stickers. She gave 27 of
   them to Franco. How many airplane stickers does
   Sally have now?

Ongoing Review

2. There are 17 pennies in all.
   How many are hidden?

   (A) 14

   (B) 13

   (C) 11

   (D) 6

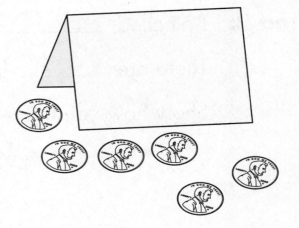

Pinching Objects

Fill a cup with 100 small objects. You could use paper clips, toothpicks, beans, pennies, or buttons. For each round, pinch some of the objects to remove them from the cup. Count how many you pinched. Figure out how many are left.

NOTE Students practice subtracting amounts from 100.

SMH 73–75

Use the 100 chart if you need it.

Round 1: I pinched _____. Equation: _____

There are _____ left in the cup.

Show how you figured out how many are left.

Round 2: I pinched _____. Equation: _____

There are _____ left in the cup.

Show how you figured out how many are left.

Story Problems (page 1 of 2)

Write an equation. Solve the problem.
Show your work.

1. Franco had 45 pennies on the table. He put 27 of them in his piggy bank. How many were still on the table?

2. Franco and Jake were playing *Cover Up* with 30 counters. Franco hid some of the counters. He left 16 showing. How many counters did Franco hide?

Story Problems (page 2 of 2)

Write an equation. Solve the problem.
Show your work.

3. Sally had 41 rainbow stickers. She gave 16 of them to Franco. How many rainbow stickers does Sally have now?

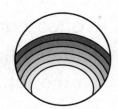

4. There were 53 cherries in a bowl. Kira ate 17 of them. How many cherries were left?

The Missing Fruit Mystery

Solve each problem. Show your work.

NOTE Students practice subtracting amounts from 100.

SMH 73–75

100 bananas   100 bananas

100 apples   100 apples

1. How many bananas are in the box? _____

How many bananas are missing? _____

2. How many apples are in the box? _____

How many apples are missing? _____

Ongoing Review

3. Mom is 34, Dad is 35, Jake is 7, and Grandma is 58. Who is older than Mom and younger than Grandma?

(A) Mom   (B) Dad   (C) Jake   (D) Grandma

More Story Problems (page 1 of 2)

Write an equation. Solve the problem.
Show your work.

1. Jake had 52 pennies. He spent 24 pennies on a new pencil. How many pennies does he have left?

2. Sally needs to climb 43 stairs to get to the top of the tower. She has climbed 28 stairs. How many more stairs does she need to climb to get to the top?

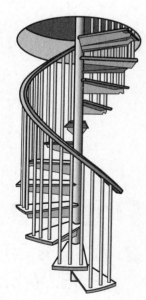

More Story Problems (page 2 of 2)

Write an equation. Solve the problem.
Show your work.

3. Kira and Sally were playing *Cover Up* with
52 counters. Kira hid some of the counters.
She left 29 showing. How many counters did
Kira hide?

4. Franco had 55 marbles. He gave his brother
27 marbles. How many marbles does Franco
have now?

Frog Stickers

Solve the problem. Show your work.

NOTE Students solve a story problem about groups of 10.

SMH 39

1. Mr. Day has 113 frog stickers. He wants to give 10 frog stickers to each student. How many students will get 10 stickers? Are there any stickers left over?

Ongoing Review

2. Kira has 1 quarter, 3 dimes, 2 nickels, and 6 pennies. How much money does she have?

(A) 56¢   (B) 66¢   (C) 71¢   (D) 81¢

Paper Clip Problems (page 1 of 2)

Write an equation. Solve the problem.
Show your work.

NOTE Students solve related story problems about subtracting amounts from 100.

SMH 71–72, 73–75

1. There were 100 paper clips in a box. On his first turn, Jake pinched 13 paper clips. How many paper clips were still in the box?

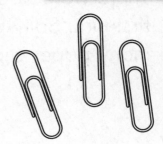

2. Jake put all of the paper clips back into the box so that he had 100. On his second turn, he pinched 14 paper clips. How many paper clips were still in the box?

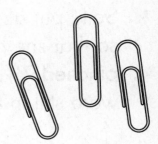

How can you use the first problem to help you solve this problem?

Paper Clip Problems (page 2 of 2)

Write an equation. Solve the problem.
Show your work.

3. There were 100 paper clips in a box. On her first turn, Sally pinched 75 paper clips. How many paper clips were still in the box?

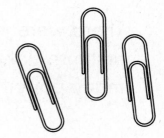

4. Sally put all of the paper clips back into the box so that she had 100. On her second turn, she pinched 74 paper clips. How many paper clips were still in the box?

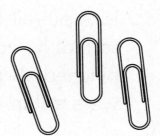

How can you use the first problem to help you solve this problem?

Pennies and Stickers (page 1 of 2)

Write an equation. Solve the problem.
Show your work.

1. Jake had 72 pennies. He spent 58 on a new pencil. How many pennies does he have left?

2. Kira had 86 sun stickers. She gave 53 of them to her sister. How many sun stickers does Kira have now?

Pennies and Stickers (page 2 of 2)

Write a story that matches the problem.
Solve the problem. Show your work.

3. 65 − 38 = _____

_____

_____

_____

4.   62
       −45

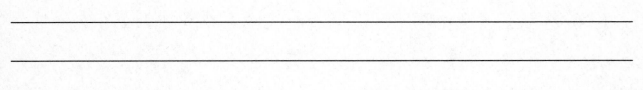

_____

_____

_____

Picking Blueberries

Write an equation. Solve the problem.
Show your work.

NOTE Students use addition or subtraction to solve two story problems.

SMH **71–72, 78–80**

1. Sally needs 100 blueberries to fill her basket. She has picked 47 blueberries. How many more does she need to pick to fill the basket?

2. Jake picked 54 blueberries. He used 38 of them to make blueberry muffins. How many blueberries does he have now?

Ongoing Review

3. How many more students have a dog than have a cat?

(A) 3   (C) 6

(B) 5   (D) 9

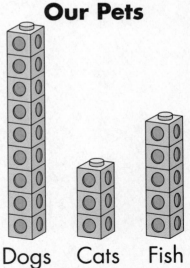

Our Pets

Dogs   Cats   Fish

Stickers to Share

Write an equation. Solve the problem.
Show your work.

NOTE Students solve subtraction story problems.

SMH 71–72

1. Jake had 82 butterfly stickers. He gave 46 of them to Sally. How many butterfly stickers does he have left?

2. Sally had 71 basketball stickers. She gave 33 of them to Kira. How many basketball stickers does she have left?

What Is the Fraction?

What fraction of the flag is gray? Black? White?
Write the fraction for each color.

NOTE Students use what they know about fractions to determine how much of a flag is shaded a certain color.

SMH 86, 87

1. 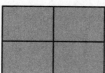   Gray: _____

2.    Gray: _____

Black: _____

White: _____

3.    Black: _____

White: _____

4.    Black: _____

White: _____

Gray: _____

5. 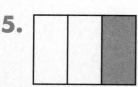   White: _____

Gray: _____

Addition Problems, Set 1 (page 1 of 2)

Write an equation. Solve the problem.
Show your work.

1. Kira had 48 balloons. Jake gave her 33
   more balloons. How many balloons does
   Kira have now?

2. Use a different strategy to solve this problem.
   Show your work.

Addition Problems, Set 1 (page 2 of 2)

Write a story that matches the equation. Solve the problem. Show your work.

3. $44 + 26 =$ _____

_____

_____

_____

_____

4. Use a different strategy to solve this problem. Show your work.

Addition Problems, Set 2 (page 1 of 2)

Write an equation. Solve the problem.
Show your work.

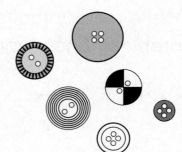

1. Franco had a collection of 57 buttons. He
   bought 34 more buttons. How many buttons
   does he have now?

2. Use a different strategy to solve this problem.
   Show your work.

Addition Problems, Set 2 (page 2 of 2)

Write a story that matches the equation. Solve the problem. Show your work.

3.   14
       +49
       ____

_____

_____

_____

_____

4. Use a different strategy to solve this problem. Show your work.

What Time Is It?

Read each clock. Record what time it is and write the time in words. Then record and draw what time it will be in 2 hours and write the time in words.

NOTE Students practice telling, recording, and determining the time to the hour and the half hour.

SMH 139, 141

What time is it now?	What time will it be in 2 hours?
 8:00 eight o'clock	 :
 :	 :
 :	 :
 :	 :
 3:00	 :

What Time Is It?

NOTE Students write the time shown on clocks and then draw hands on clocks to show time.

Write the time shown on each clock.

Show each time on the clock.

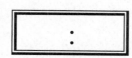

:

2 : 20

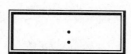

:

4 : 35

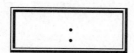

:

7 : 50

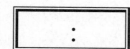

:

10 : 00

Addition at Home (page 1 of 2)

Write an equation. Solve the problem.
Show your work.

NOTE As students solve two story problems, they write equations, add 2-digit numbers, and find different ways to solve a problem.

SMH 63–66

1. Jake had 39 pennies. His mother gave him 22 more pennies. How many pennies does he have now?

2. Use a different strategy to solve this problem. Show your work.

Addition at Home (page 2 of 2)

Write an equation. Solve the problem.
Show your work.

3. Sally had 24 stamps. Jake gave her 67 more stamps. How many stamps does she have now?

4. Use a different strategy to solve this problem.
Show your work.

Addition Problems, Set 3 (page 1 of 2)

Write an equation. Try to solve the problem by keeping one number whole. Show your work.

1. Kira counted 49 ladybugs on the tree and 28 ladybugs on the ground. How many ladybugs did Kira count?

2. Franco had 66 car stickers. Jake gave him 52 car stickers. How many car stickers does Franco have now?

Addition Problems, Set 3 (page 2 of 2)

Write a story that matches each problem.
Solve the problems. Show your work.

3.   55
      +36

_____

_____

_____

4. 17 + 62 = _____

_____

_____

_____

Going to the Movies

Write an equation. Try to solve the problem by keeping one number whole. Show your work.

NOTE As students solve two story problems, they write equations, add 2-digit numbers, and find different ways to solve a problem.

SMH 63–66

1. On Monday, 38 people went to a scary movie. 56 people went to a funny movie. How many people went to the movies on Monday?

2. On Tuesday, 23 people went to a dinosaur movie. 49 people went to a shark movie. How many people went to the movies on Tuesday?

Ongoing Review

3. Which combination does **not** make 100?

   Ⓐ 90 + 9   Ⓑ 80 + 20   Ⓒ 70 + 30   Ⓓ 60 + 40

Writing Stories (page 1 of 2)

Write a story that matches the problem.
Solve the problem. Show your work.

> **NOTE** Students write stories that match the given problems and practice adding 2-digit numbers.
>
> **SMH** 63–66

1. 37 + 48 = _____

_____

_____

_____

_____

2. Use a different strategy to solve this problem.
Show your work.

Writing Stories (page 2 of 2)

Write a story that matches the problem. Solve the problem. Show your work.

3.   63
    +29

_____

_____

_____

_____

4. Use a different strategy to solve this problem. Show your work.

Addition Problems, Set 4 (page 1 of 2)

Write a story that matches the problem. Try to
solve the problem by adding tens and ones.
Show your work.

1.   27
        +65

_____

_____

_____

2. 42 + 53 = _____

_____

_____

_____

Addition Problems, Set 4 (page 2 of 2)

Write an equation. Try to solve each problem by keeping one number whole. Show your work.

3. Jake had 88 paper clips. He found 16 more paper clips in the hall. How many paper clips does Jake have now?

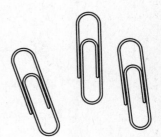

4. Sally had 73 marbles. Franco gave her 25 marbles. How many marbles does Sally have now?

Today's Number: 12

Today's Number is <u>12</u>.

NOTE Students write expressions that equal Today's Number by using only subtraction. There are many possible solutions.

SMH 55

$$42 - 30$$
$$50 - 20 - 10 - 8$$
$$12 - 0$$

1. Write at least five different ways to make Today's Number. Use only subtraction.

Ongoing Review

2. What time will it be in three hours?

(A) 3:45   (C) 6:45

(B) 5:45   (D) 12:45

More Addition at Home (page 1 of 2)

Write an equation. Solve the problem. Show your work.

NOTE As students solve two story problems, they write equations, add 2-digit numbers, and find different ways to solve a problem.

SMH **63–66**

1. Sally had 48 skateboard stickers. Her brother gave her 36 more skateboard stickers. How many does she have now?

2. Use a different strategy to solve this problem. Show your work.

More Addition at Home (page 2 of 2)

Write an equation. Solve the problem.
Show your work.

3. Franco had 63 truck stickers. Kira gave him 34 more. How many truck stickers does he have now?

4. Use a different strategy to solve this problem. Show your work.

Addition Problems, Set 5 (page 1 of 2)

Write an equation. Solve the problem.
Show your work.

1. Kira had 69 beads. Jake gave her 19 more beads to make a necklace. How many beads does she have now?

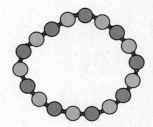

2. Franco counted 46 pretzels in his bowl. Sally counted 58 pretzels in her bowl. How many pretzels do they have in all?

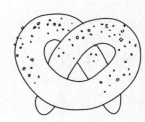

Addition Problems, Set 5 (page 2 of 2)

Write a story that matches each problem.
Solve the problems. Show your work.

3.   41
     +74
     ____

_____

_____

_____

4. 64 + 35 = _____

_____

_____

_____

More Subtracting Tens

Solve these problems. Fill in
the totals on the 100 chart below.

NOTE Students practice subtracting 10
and multiples of 10 from any number.

SMH 24

1. 83 – 10 – 10 – 20 = _____

2. 94 – 30 – 10 = _____

3. 85 – 40 – 10 – 20 = _____

4. 79 – 20 – 10 = _____

5. 91 – 50 – 10 – 10 = _____

6. 32 – 20 – 10 = _____

7. 67 – 10 – 10 – 30 = _____

8. 58 – 30 = _____

9. Fill in the other missing numbers on the 100 chart.

1		3				7			
11			14						20
				25	26				
	32				36		38	39	
41			44			47			
	52			55			58		
61			64	65			68		70
		73				77		79	
81	82				86				90
			94					99	

Evens, Odds, and Combinations (page 1 of 2)

Solve each problem. Show your work.

NOTE Students review what they know about adding odd and even numbers and practice two of the remaining addition combinations.

SMH 41–42, 53

1. There are 13 girls and 11 boys in Ms. Wong's class. They are going to play a game in pairs. Will everyone have a partner?

2. There are 17 boys and 13 girls on the playground. They are going to play a game of soccer. Can they make two equal teams?

Evens, Odds, and Combinations (page 2 of 2)

Solve each problem. Show your work.

3. Kira has trouble with 7 + 9. Write a clue that will help Kira remember 7 + 9.

$$9 + 7 =$$

$$7 + 9 =$$

Clue: _____

4. Franco has trouble with 8 + 6. Write a clue that will help Franco remember 8 + 6.

$$6 + 8 =$$

$$8 + 6 =$$

Clue: _____

Prize Tickets (page 1 of 2)

At the spring fair, Robin wins
200 prize tickets.

NOTE Students solve real-world
problems involving the math
content of this unit.

1. Which prizes could she get
with 100 tickets?

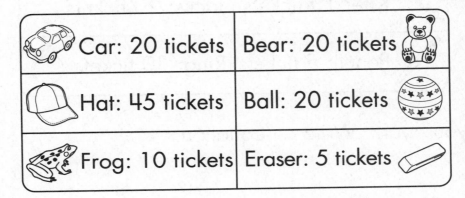

Car: 20 tickets	Bear: 20 tickets
Hat: 45 tickets	Ball: 20 tickets
Frog: 10 tickets	Eraser: 5 tickets

Show your work. Write an equation.

Prize Tickets (page 2 of 2)

2. Which of these prizes could Robin get with the other 100 tickets?

Yo-yo: 25 tickets Windmill: 15 tickets

Kite: 10 tickets Jacks: 20 tickets

Pencil: 5 tickets Ring: 30 tickets

Show your work. Write an equation.

Combining Sets of Stickers (page 1 of 2)

Problem 1

Kira has 135 stickers.

Sticker notation:

James has 123 stickers.

Sticker notation:

Equation:

Equation:

If Kira and James combine their sets, how many stickers will they have?

Problem 2

Sally has 250 stickers.

Sticker notation:

Franco has 248 stickers.

Sticker notation:

Equation:

Equation:

If Sally and Franco combine their sets, how many stickers will they have?

Combining Sets of Stickers (page 2 of 2)

Problem 3

Sally has 307 stickers.

Kira has 211 stickers.
Sticker notation:

Sticker notation:

Equation:

Equation:

If Sally and Kira combine their sets, how many stickers will they have?

Problem 4

James has 500 stickers.

Franco has 391 stickers.
Sticker notation:

Sticker notation:

Equation:

Equation:

If James and Franco combine their sets, how many stickers will they have?

Plus or Minus 10

Write the number that is 10 more or 10 less than the target number.

NOTE Students practice adding 10 to and subtracting 10 from a given number.

10 Less	Target Number	10 More
	126	
	259	
	330	
	418	
	489	
	507	
	590	
	677	
	795	
	803	
	990	

Hundreds, Tens, and Ones

NOTE Students practice representing numbers using sticker notation and as the sum of hundreds, tens, and ones.

For each number, represent the amount using sticker notation. Then record an equation that shows the number of hundreds, tens, and ones.

Example: 127

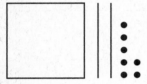

$127 = \underline{100} + \underline{20} + \underline{7}$

183 $183 = \underline{} + \underline{} + \underline{}$	235 $235 = \underline{} + \underline{} + \underline{}$
318 $318 = \underline{} + \underline{} + \underline{}$	456 $456 = \underline{} + \underline{} + \underline{}$
702 $702 = \underline{} + \underline{} + \underline{}$	851 $851 = \underline{} + \underline{} + \underline{}$

Partners, Teams, and Paper Clips

More Sticker Problems (page 1 of 2)

Problem 1

Josh has 147 stickers.

Sticker notation:

Equation:

Jake has 115 stickers.

Sticker notation:

Equation:

If Josh and Jake combine their sets, how many stickers will they have?

Sticker notation:

Equation:

Problem 2

Sally has 258 stickers.

Sticker notation:

Equation:

Franco has 133 stickers.

Sticker notation:

Equation:

If Sally and Franco combine their sets, how many stickers will they have?

Sticker notation:

Equation:

Partners, Teams, and Paper Clips

More Sticker Problems (page 2 of 2)

Problem 3

Sally has 409 stickers.
Sticker
notation:

Equation:

Kira has 231 stickers.
Sticker
notation:

Equation:

If Sally and Kira combine their sets,
how many stickers will they have?

Sticker notation:

Equation:

Problem 4

James has 570 stickers.
Sticker
notation:

Equation:

Franco has 341 stickers.
Sticker
notation:

Equation:

If James and Franco combine their sets,
how many stickers will they have?

Sticker notation:

Equation:

Number Strips (page 1 of 2)

Write the missing numbers on the counting strips.

NOTE Students practice skip counting by 2s, 5s, and 10s.

112		160
114		
	125	140
		130
122	140	
124	145	
		90

Number Strips (page 2 of 2)

Write the missing numbers on the counting strips.

375	988	660
385		
	992	680
415		
		720
	1,002	

Session 5A.2

Practicing with Subtraction Cards

Choose 6 Subtraction Card problems from your "working on" pile, and write these on the blank cards below. Practice these subtraction facts.

____ – ____ = ____ Addition Clue: _____	____ – ____ = ____ Addition Clue: _____
____ – ____ = ____ Addition Clue: _____	____ – ____ = ____ Addition Clue: _____
____ – ____ = ____ Addition Clue: _____	____ – ____ = ____ Addition Clue: _____

Subtracting Groups of Stickers (page 1 of 2)

Write an equation and use stickers to represent each problem.

Problem 1

Sally had a collection of 176 star stickers. She decided to give 115 of these stickers to Franco for his collection. How many star stickers did Sally have left?

Equation: _____ – _____ = _____ stickers

Sticker notation:

Problem 2

Jake collects car stickers. He has 264 car stickers in his collection. He decides to give 120 of them to James. How many car stickers does Jake have left in his collection?

Equation: _____ – _____ = _____ stickers

Sticker notation:

Subtracting Groups of Stickers (page 2 of 2)

Write an equation and use stickers to represent each problem.

Problem 3

Kira wanted to start a collection of cat stickers. Sally had 388 cat stickers in her sticker book. She gave 150 of them to Kira for her new collection. How many cat stickers does Sally have now?

Equation: _____ – _____ = _____ stickers

Sticker notation:

Problem 4

Franco decided to count all of the stickers in his collection and then put them in sticker books. Franco counted 680 stickers. On Saturday, he put 350 stickers into sticker books. How many stickers does Franco have left to put into sticker books?

Equation: _____ – _____ = _____ stickers

Sticker notation:

Plus or Minus 100

> **NOTE** Students practice adding and subtracting 100 from a given number.

Write the number that is 100 more or 100 less than the target number.

100 Less	Target Number	100 More
	150	
	276	
	383	
	195	
	400	
	711	
	528	
	632	
	949	
	855	
	900	

More Sticker Problems (page 1 of 2)

Write an equation and use stickers to represent each problem.

Problem 1

Sally bought a sticker book to keep her stickers in. She has 770 stickers to put in the book. She put 248 stickers in her book. How many does she have left to do?

Equation: _____ – _____ = _____ stickers

Sticker notation:

Problem 2

Franco and Kira decided to combine their sticker collections. When they counted, they had 8 sheets of 100, 6 strips of 10, and 4 singles. How many stickers did they have in all?

Equation: _____ + _____ + _____ = _____ stickers

Sticker notation:

Of these stickers, Kira decided to give 255 to her sister. How many stickers do Franco and Kira have left? (You can use the sticker notation above to show your work.)

Equation: _____ – _____ = _____ stickers

More Sticker Problems (page 2 of 2)

Problem 3

Write a sticker problem to go with the following equation:
736 − 361 = ____

_____

_____

_____

Solve the problem. Show your work with sticker notation and equations.

Problem 4

Sally has this many stickers in her collection:

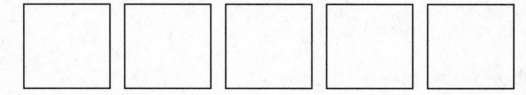

Sally gave 156 stickers to Kira for helping her babysit her little brother. How many stickers does Sally have left?

Equation: ____ − ____ = ____ stickers

Solve the problem. Show your work.

Fraction Practice (page 1 of 2)

NOTE Students divide shapes into equal parts.

1. Find three different ways to divide these rectangles into fourths.

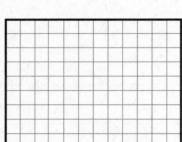   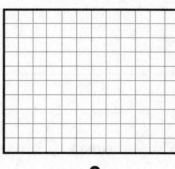   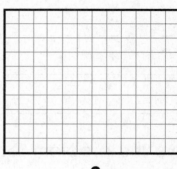

     1   **2**   **3**

2. In Rectangle 1, color $\frac{1}{4}$ blue, $\frac{1}{4}$ red, and $\frac{1}{4}$ green.

What fraction of the rectangle is colored? _____

What fraction of the rectangle is **not** colored? _____

3. In Rectangle 2, color $\frac{1}{2}$ green and $\frac{1}{4}$ red.

How many fourths are green? _____

4. In Rectangle 3, color $\frac{1}{4}$ red, $\frac{1}{2}$ green, and $\frac{1}{4}$ blue.

What fraction of the rectangle is colored? _____

Fraction Practice (page 2 of 2)

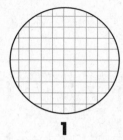 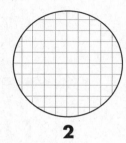 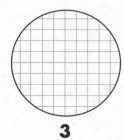 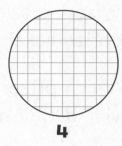

    1   **2**   **3**   **4**

5. Divide Circle 1 into halves. Label each half with a fraction.

6. Divide Circle 2 into fourths. Color $\frac{1}{2}$ red and $\frac{1}{4}$ green.

What fraction of the circle is colored? _____

What fraction of the circle is **not** colored? _____

7. Divide Circle 3 into fourths. Decide how to color it using red, blue, and green. Then record the fractions of each color.

What fraction of the circle is blue? _____

What fraction of the circle is green? _____

What fraction of the circle is red? _____

8. Challenge How can you divide Circle 4 into 8 equal parts? Color the circle using red, blue, and green. Then record the fractions of each color.

_____ of the circle is blue.

_____ of the circle is green.

_____ of the circle is red.

Prize Tickets (page 1 of 2)

At the spring fair, Robin wins
200 prize tickets.

NOTE Students solve real-world problems involving the math content of this unit.

1. Which prizes could she get
with 100 tickets?

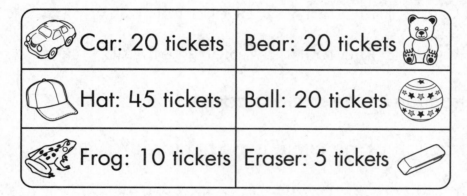

Car: 20 tickets	Bear: 20 tickets
Hat: 45 tickets	Ball: 20 tickets
Frog: 10 tickets	Eraser: 5 tickets

Show your work. Write an equation.

Prize Tickets (page 2 of 2)

2. Which of these prizes could Robin get with the other 100 tickets?

Yo-yo: 25 tickets	Windmill: 15 tickets
Kite: 10 tickets	Jacks: 20 tickets
Pencil: 5 tickets	Ring: 30 tickets

Show your work. Write an equation.

Complicated Kris Northern

"This image illustrates some of the best qualities of fractals—infinity, reiteration, and self similarity." – **Kris Northern**

Investigations
IN NUMBER, DATA, AND SPACE®

Measuring Length and Time

Practicing with Subtraction Cards

NOTE Students practice subtraction facts. Ask your child to explain how the addition clues help him or her remember these subtraction facts.

Choose 6 Subtraction Card problems from your "working on" pile, and write these on the blank cards below. Practice these at home with a friend or family member.

___ − ___ = ___

Addition Clue: _____

___ − ___ = ___

Addition Clue: _____

___ − ___ = ___

Addition Clue: _____

___ − ___ = ___

Addition Clue: _____

___ − ___ = ___

Addition Clue: _____

___ − ___ = ___

Addition Clue: _____

Fraction Flags

Write what fraction of the flag each color is.

NOTE Students use what they know about fractions to determine how much of a flag is shaded a certain color.

 SMH 84–87

1. Black: _____

    White: _____

2. Gray: _____

    White: _____

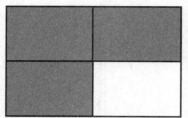

3. Gray: _____

    White: _____

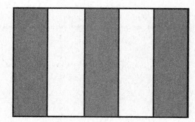

4. Black: _____

    White: _____

5. Black: _____

    White: _____

    Gray: _____

Scavenger Hunt 1: Measuring Lengths (page 1 of 2)

Find things that are about the same length as each paper strip.

Strip A	Strip B
Strip C	**Strip D**

Scavenger Hunt 1: Measuring Lengths (page 2 of 2) WRITING

Find things that are about the same length as each paper strip.

Strip E	Strip F

Write about how you compared objects to the paper strips.

_____

_____

_____

_____

_____

Ways to Get to 100

NOTE Students combine numbers to make 100 and write equations that have more than two addends (the numbers being added).

SMH 54

1. $10 + \underline{\hspace{1cm}} + \underline{\hspace{1cm}} + \underline{\hspace{1cm}} = 100$

2. $27 + \underline{\hspace{1cm}} + \underline{\hspace{1cm}} + \underline{\hspace{1cm}} = 100$

3. $14 + \underline{\hspace{1cm}} + \underline{\hspace{1cm}} + \underline{\hspace{1cm}} = 100$

4. $34 + \underline{\hspace{1cm}} + \underline{\hspace{1cm}} + \underline{\hspace{1cm}} = 100$

5. $22 + \underline{\hspace{1cm}} + \underline{\hspace{1cm}} + \underline{\hspace{1cm}} = 100$

6. $8 + \underline{\hspace{1cm}} + \underline{\hspace{1cm}} + \underline{\hspace{1cm}} = 100$

7. $11 + \underline{\hspace{1cm}} + \underline{\hspace{1cm}} + \underline{\hspace{1cm}} = 100$

Scavenger Hunt 2: How Many Paper Strips? (page 1 of 2)

Find an object to match each length.

Blue Strips	Yellow Strips
Find something 3 blue strips long. Object: _____	How many yellow strips is the object? Estimate: _____ Measure: _____
Find something 2 blue strips long. Object: _____	How many yellow strips is the object? Estimate: _____ Measure: _____
Find something 5 blue strips long. Object: _____	How many yellow strips is the object? Estimate: _____ Measure: _____
Find something 4 blue strips long. Object: _____	How many yellow strips is the object? Estimate: _____ Measure: _____

Scavenger Hunt 2:
How Many Paper Strips? (page 2 of 2)

Blue Strips	Yellow Strips
Find something 6 blue strips long. Object: _____	How many yellow strips is the object? Estimate: _____ Measure: _____
Find something 7 blue strips long. Object: _____	How many yellow strips is the object? Estimate: _____ Measure: _____
Find something 10 blue strips long. Object: _____	How many yellow strips is the object? Estimate: _____ Measure: _____

What did you notice about the number of blue strips compared to the number of yellow strips?

_____

_____

How Many Strips?

A class measured with red and green paper strips. All the red strips were the same length. All the green strips were the same length. Use the measurements for the teacher's desk to figure out the missing measurements.

> **NOTE** Students look at measurements to find the relationship between different units.
>
> SMH 150–151

Object	Measurement in Red Strips	Measurement in Green Strips
1. Teacher's desk	10 red strips	5 green strips
2. Student's desk	4 red strips	_____ green strips
3. Chalkboard	26 red strips	_____ green strips
4. Dictionary	_____ red strips	1 green strip
5. Aquarium	_____ red strips	4 green strips

Ongoing Review

6. $17 +$ _____ $= 22$

(A) 7   (B) 9   (C) 3   (D) 5

Scavenger Hunt at Home (page 1 of 2)

NOTE Students measure objects with measuring strips of different but related lengths.

SMH 147, 150–151

Find an object to match each length.

Blue Strips	Yellow Strips
Find something 3 blue strips long. Object: _____	How many yellow strips is the object? Estimate: _____ Measure: _____
Find something 2 blue strips long. Object: _____	How many yellow strips is the object? Estimate: _____ Measure: _____
Find something 5 blue strips long. Object: _____	How many yellow strips is the object? Estimate: _____ Measure: _____
Find something 4 blue strips long. Object: _____	How many yellow strips is the object? Estimate: _____ Measure: _____

Scavenger Hunt at Home (page 2 of 2)

Find an object to match each length.

Blue Strips	Yellow Strips
Find something 6 blue strips long. Object: _____	How many yellow strips is the object? Estimate: _____ Measure: _____
Find something 7 blue strips long. Object: _____	How many yellow strips is the object? Estimate: _____ Measure: _____
Find something 10 blue strips long. Object: _____	How many yellow strips is the object? Estimate: _____ Measure: _____

What did you notice about the number of blue strips compared to the number of yellow strips?

_____

_____

How Far Can You Jump?

Jump like a frog, a rabbit, and a kid. Measure each jump.

a frog jump   a rabbit jump   a kid jump

_____   _____   _____

1. What unit did you use to measure your jumps? _____

2. Which jump is the longest? _____ How long is it? _____

3. Which jump is the shortest? _____ How long is it? _____

4. How many units longer is your longest jump

than your shortest jump? _____

5. Explain how you solved the problem.

_____

_____

Name Date

Time to the Quarter Hour

Read each clock. Record what time it is. Then, show what time it will be in 1 hour and record that time.

NOTE Students practice telling time, determining what time it will be in one hour, and recording time using both analog and digital notation.

SMH **135, 138, 140, 141**

What time is it now?		What time will it be in 1 hour?	
	:		:
	:		:
	:		:
	:		:
	:		:

Measuring at Home

1. Use your measuring strips
to measure objects at home.

NOTE Students use measuring strips
to measure objects at home. They then
solve a comparison measuring problem.

SMH 150–151

Name of Object	Number of Blue Strips	Number of Yellow Strips

2. Kira was measuring at home. The TV measured
32 cubes. The table measured 54 cubes. How
much longer is the table than the TV?

Solve the problem. Show your work.

How Many Blue Strips?
How Many Yellow Strips?

Solve the problems. Show your work.

1. If the shelf is 12 blue strips long, how many yellow strips long is it?

2. If the rug is 22 yellow strips long, how many blue strips long is it?

3. If the bulletin board is 20 blue strips long, how many yellow strips long is it?

4. If the door is 32 yellow strips high, how many blue strips high is it?

Two "100" Stories

Finish the story to make 100.

NOTE Students practice adding several numbers and determine how far the sums are from 100.

SMH 54, 79–80

1. Sarah collected 100 cans last week.

On Monday, she collected 15 cans.

On Tuesday, she collected 25 cans.

On Wednesday, she collected 7 cans.

On Thursday, she collected _____ cans.

On Friday, she collected 33 cans.

2. Antonio needs 100 coupons to get a free pizza.

He saved 32 coupons from his pizza party.

His aunt gave him 16 coupons.

Robert gave him 28 coupons.

Then his mother gave him _____.

He made it! He has 100!

Ongoing Review

3. How many total students are in Mr. Baley's class?

Students in Mr. Baley's Class	
Boys:	ЖЖ |||||
Girls:	ЖЖ ЖЖ |||||

(A) 23   (B) 22   (C) 21   (D) 19

Measuring Jumps with Cubes

Measure your longest jump and your shortest jump with cubes.

1. My longest jump is _____ cubes.

2. My shortest jump is _____ cubes.

3. How many cubes longer is your longest jump than your shortest jump? Solve the problem and show how you solved it.

4. Write an equation that shows your answer.

A Jumping Contest

The students in Room 203 held a grasshopper-jumping contest. They recorded the length of each jump.

NOTE Students compare measurements, find the shortest and longest, and find the difference between shortest and longest.

Grasshopper	Length of Jump
Group A's grasshopper	36 cubes
Group B's grasshopper	42 cubes
Group C's grasshopper	25 cubes
Group D's grasshopper	57 cubes

1. Which group's grasshopper had the longest jump? _____

2. Which group's grasshopper had the shortest jump? _____

3. How many cubes longer was the longest jump than the shortest jump? _____

4. If the students had only 40 cubes, how could they have measured Group D's grasshopper's jump?

_____

_____

How Much Longer?

Use the information from your class to fill in the blanks.

1. The longest jump in the class was _____ cubes.

2. The shortest jump in the class was _____ cubes.

3. Write an equation.

How much longer was the longest jump than the shortest?
Solve the problem.

Today's Number: 25

Circle all of the problems that equal Today's Number.

NOTE Students determine if different expressions of numbers are equal to 25.

SMH 55

Today's Number is 25.

$50 - 20 - 5$	$10 + 5 + 10 + 5$
$6 + 4 + 7 + 3 + 4 + 1$	$75 - 55$
$8 + 6 + 2 + 5 + 4$	$100 - 10 - 10 - 50 - 5$
$85 - 60 - 5$	$7 + 7 + 6 + 3 + 2$
$35 - 15$	$100 - 25 - 25 - 25$

Jumping in the Land of Inch

Use inch-bricks to figure out how far each of the athletes jumped.

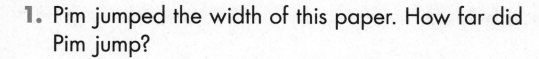

1. Pim jumped the width of this paper. How far did Pim jump?

2. Ren jumped the length of a craft stick. How far did Ren jump?

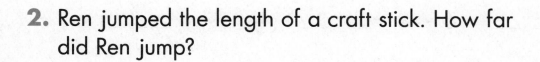

3. Hap jumped the length of this paper. How far did Hap jump?

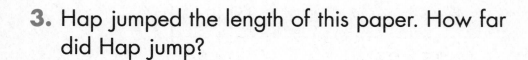

4. Tob jumped the length of a glue stick. How far did Tob jump?

Addition Combinations and Sequencing Numbers

NOTE Students practice solving addition combinations and sequencing numbers from 1–100.

SMH 24, 43

1. Solve these problems. Fill in the totals on the 100 Chart below.

8 + 8 = _____   9 + 3 = _____   7 + 2 = _____

9 + 7 = _____   7 + 4 = _____   9 + 9 = _____

8 + 7 = _____   9 + 6 = _____   8 + 9 = _____

7 + 7 = _____   6 + 8 = _____   4 + 9 = _____

2. Fill in the other missing numbers on the 100 chart.

	2				6	7			
								19	
21				25	26				30
	33					37		39	
	42		44		46			49	50
	53		55						
61							68		
71			74		76			79	80
	82			85			88		
91	92	93			96				

NOTE Students combine two numbers to determine the total number of stickers.

Combining Sets of Stickers (page 1 of 2)

For each problem, use sticker notation, and write an equation that represents each set of stickers.

Problem 1

Kira has 218 stickers. Sticker notation:	James has 360 stickers. Sticker notation:
Equation:	Equation:

If Kira and James combine their sets, how many stickers will they have in all?

Combining Sets of Stickers

(page 2 of 2)

For each problem, use sticker notation, and write an equation that represents each set of stickers.

Problem 2

| Sally has 307 stickers.
Sticker notation:

Equation: | Franco has 406 stickers.
Sticker notation:

Equation: |

If Sally and Franco combine their sets, how many stickers will they have in all?

Clothes in the Land of Inch (page 1 of 2)

Measure each object with an inch-brick measuring
tool. Record each length.

1. The length of Princess Funer's cloak is the same
   as the length of your pencil.

   How many inch-bricks is Princess Funer's cloak? _____

2. The length of Ren's jacket is the same as the
   length of 9 cubes.

   How many inch-bricks is Ren's jacket? _____

3. The length of Pim's shirtsleeve is the same as the
   length of 2 craft sticks.

   How many inch-bricks is Pim's shirt sleeve? _____

4. The length of Raf's knee sock is the same as the
   length of 4 cubes.

   How many inch-bricks is Raf's knee sock? _____

5. The length of Nim's pants is the same as the
   length of 4 color tiles.

   How many inch-bricks are Nim's pants? _____

Clothes in the Land of Inch (page 2 of 2)

6. The height of the king's crown is the same as the length of 3 color tiles.

How many inch-bricks high is the king's crown? _____

7. The length of Gar's jacket is the same as the length of 8 color tiles.

How many inch-bricks is Gar's jacket? _____

Use the information above to solve each problem. Show your work.

8. How many more inch-bricks is Ren's jacket than Raf's knee sock?

9. How many more inch-bricks is Gar's jacket than the king's crown?

10. How many more inch-bricks are Nim's pants than the king's crown?

Buildings in the Land of Inch (page 1 of 2)

Use your inch-brick measuring tool to answer each question.

1. The people in the Land of Inch grow to be about as tall as the inch-brick measuring tool. How many inch-bricks tall are the people in the Land of Inch?

2. Princess Funer's castle is about as long as the table. How many inch-bricks long is Princess Funer's castle?

3. Tob's house is about as wide as your desk. How many inch-bricks wide is Tob's house?

Buildings in the Land of Inch (page 2 of 2)

4. Ren's house is about as tall as the seat of your chair. How many inch-bricks tall is Ren's house?

5. Pim's house is about as tall as your desk. How many inch-bricks tall is Pim's house?

6. Gar's house is about as tall as the doorknob is from the floor. How many inch-bricks tall is Gar's house?

7. The king's castle is about as tall as the bookcase. How many inch-bricks tall is the king's castle?

Children's Jumps in the Land of Inch (page 1 of 2)

The children of inch measured their jumps, too.
Use your inch-brick measuring tool to find how
far they jumped.

1. Bok's jump was as long as 3 cubes. Draw a line
   the length of Bok's jump.

   How many inch-bricks was Bok's jump? _____

2. Gar's jump was as long as a marker. Draw a
   line the length of Gar's jump.

   How many inch-bricks was Gar's jump? _____

3. Who jumped farther, Bok or Gar? How much
   farther did he jump? Show your work.

Children's Jumps in the Land of Inch (page 2 of 2)

4. Raf's jump was as long as a craft stick. Draw a line the length of Raf's jump.

How many inch-bricks was Raf's jump? _____

5. Nim's jump was as long as $3\frac{1}{2}$ tiles. Draw a line the length of Nim's jump.

How many inch-bricks was Nim's jump? _____

6. Who jumped farther, Raf or Nim? How much farther did he jump? Show your work.

Missing Numbers

Write the missing numbers on the counting strips.

NOTE Students practice counting by 2s, 5s and 10s.

 26, 35–39

126		**130**
128	**95**	**120**
	100	
132		
		90
	115	

NOTE Students use inches to measure objects at home.

SMH 147

Measuring with Inch-Bricks at Home

Use your inch-bricks to measure things at home. If you want, glue the inch-bricks onto the measuring tool below.

1. Find something that is 6 inch-bricks long.

What is it? _____

2. Find something that is 3 inch-bricks long.

What is it? _____

3. How long is your toothpaste tube? _____

4. How long is a bar of soap? _____

5. How long is a spoon? _____

Measuring Tool:

Missing Numbers

NOTE Students practice counting by 2s, 5s, and 10s.

Write the missing numbers on the counting strips.

230	485	880
232	490	890
	505	
240		930
	515	

Paths in the Land of Inch

The king's castle is in a corner of the Land of Inch. Use the directions below to create your map of the Land of Inch.

1. The path from the king's castle to his garden is 15 inch-bricks long. Show on your map the length of the path from the king's castle to his garden.

2. The path from the king's castle to Princess Funer's castle is 25 inch-bricks long. Show on your map the length of the path from the king's castle to Princess Funer's castle.

3. The path from the king's castle to Pim's house is 28 inch-bricks long. Show on your map the length of the path from the king's castle to Pim's house.

4. What else do you want to show on your map of the Land of Inch? Draw it on the map and show how far away it is from the king's castle.

Measuring With Pencils

Paul and Pedra measured the width of a desk. They used their pencils as the unit of measure. Here are their measurements:

NOTE Students answer questions about measurements made with different-sized units.

SMH 150–151

Paul: 32 pencils   Pedra: 46 pencils

1. Why did they get different measurements?

_____

_____

_____

2. Which pencil below is Paul's? Circle it.

Which pencil is Pedra's? Draw a line under it.

Ongoing Review

3. How many hands are there in a group of 16 people?

(A) 12   (B) 26   (C) 32   (D) 42

What Time Is It?
What Time Will It Be?

Read each clock. Record the time. Then show what time it will be in 2 hours and record that time.

> **NOTE** Students practice telling time and determining what time it will be to the hour and the half hour.
>
> **SMH** 137, 139, 141

What time is it now?		What time will it be in 2 hours?	
(clock)	**7:30**	(clock)	:
(clock)	:	(clock)	:
(clock)	:	(clock)	:
(clock)	:	(clock)	:
(clock)	**9:30**	(clock)	:

Rulers and Inch-Brick Measuring Tools ✏️WRITING

Examine your ruler and your inch-brick measuring tool. Record your answers.

Name two things that are the same.

1. _____
   _____
   _____

2. _____
   _____
   _____

Name two things that are different.

1. _____
   _____
   _____

2. _____
   _____
   _____

Body Benchmarks

Body benchmarks are parts of the body that you can sometimes use to measure objects if you do not have a ruler handy. Use body benchmarks to answer each question.

1. What on your body is about 1 inch long? _____

2. What on your body is about 6 inches long? _____

3. What on your body is about 12 inches (1 foot) long? _____

4. Use your body benchmark to measure your pencil.

Estimated length: _____

Use your ruler to measure your pencil.

Measured length: _____

5. Use your body benchmark to measure the height of your chair.

Estimated height: _____

Use your ruler or a yardstick to measure the height of your chair.

Measured height: _____

Measure and Compare (page 1 of 2)

Find each of these objects in your classroom.
Use a ruler to measure each object. Record each
measurement and answer the questions.

Scissors _____

Which is longer? _____

Marker _____

How much longer is it? _____

Ruler _____

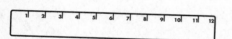

Which is longer? _____

Pencil _____

How much longer is it? _____

Length of table _____

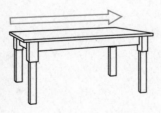

Which is longer? _____

Length of bookshelf _____

How much longer is it? _____

Measure and Compare (page 2 of 2)

Find each of these objects in your classroom.
Use a ruler to measure each object. Record each
measurement and answer the questions.

Height of chair _____   Height of table _____

Which is taller? _____   How much taller is it? _____

Width of your
reading book _____   Length of your
                                 reading book _____

Which is longer? _____   How much longer is it? _____

Width of the door _____   Width of the window _____

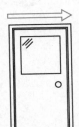   

Which is wider? _____   How much wider is it? _____

Counting Money

How much money does each student have? How much more does each one need to make $1.00?

NOTE Students practice counting money and determining the difference between the amount they count and $1.00.

SMH **19, 21**

1.

Kira has _____.

Kira needs _____ to make $1.00.

2.

Jake has _____.

Jake needs _____ to make $1.00.

3.

Franco has _____.

Franco needs _____ to make $1.00.

4.

Sally has _____.

Sally needs _____ to make $1.00.

Session 3.2

NOTE Students compare two measurements and determine the difference between them.

Comparing Measurements (page 1 of 2)

Circle the longer object. Record how much longer it is. Show your work.

1.

Length of a pencil: 6 inches

Height of a lamp: 10 inches

How much longer? _____

2.

Length of Jake's arm: 14 inches

Length of Jake's leg: 26 inches

How much longer? _____

Comparing Measurements (page 2 of 2)

3.

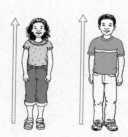

Kira's height: 48 inches

Franco's height: 53 inches

How much taller? _____

Think about all of the things listed above.

4. Which is the longest? _____

5. Which is the shortest? _____

6. What is the difference between them? _____

Measuring Our Classroom

Choose a unit to measure the length or width of your classroom.

1. Did you measure the length or width of the classroom? _____

2. What unit did you use to measure the classroom? _____

3. What was the measurement? _____

4. Describe how you measured the classroom.

_____

_____

_____

_____

_____

_____

Using Groups to Solve a Story Problem

NOTE Students use what they know about 10s and 1s to solve a story problem.

SMH 31, 35–36, 39

Mrs. Lydel has 128 star stickers. She wants to give each student 10 star stickers.

How many students can get 10 stickers?

Are there any extra stickers?

Solve the problem. Show your work.

Length and Width (page 1 of 2)

Choose four rectangular objects at home. Use body benchmarks to estimate the length and the width of each object. Then use a ruler to measure the length and width in inches.

> **NOTE** Students use body benchmarks to estimate and then a ruler to measure the length and width of 4 different objects.
>
> **SMH** 146, 155, 156

First Object

Name of the object: _____

Estimated Length: _____   Measured Length: _____

Estimated Width: _____   Measured Width: _____

Explain how you used body benchmarks to estimate.

Second Object

Name of the object: _____

Estimated Length: _____   Measured Length: _____

Estimated Width: _____   Measured Width: _____

Explain how you used body benchmarks to estimate.

Length and Width (page 2 of 2)

Third Object

Name: _____

Estimated Length: _____   Measured Length: _____

Estimated Width: _____   Measured Width: _____

Explain how you used body benchmarks to estimate.

Fourth Object

Name: _____

Estimated Length: _____   Measured Length: _____

Estimated Width: _____   Measured Width: _____

Explain how you used body benchmarks to estimate.

Subtracting Groups of Stickers

NOTE Students subtract to determine how many stickers are left.

For each problem, use sticker notation that represents each set of stickers.

Problem 1

Jake collects baseball stickers. He has 835 stickers in his collection. He decides to give 525 of them to James. How many stickers does Jake have left in his collection?

Equation:

_____ − _____ = _____ stickers

Sticker notation:

Problem 2

Sally had a collection of 352 dog stickers. She decided to give 125 of these stickers to Franco for his collection. How many dog stickers did Sally have left?

Equation:

_____ − _____ = _____ stickers

Sticker notation:

Metric Scavenger Hunt

Find things that are 1 meter long and
1 centimeter long.

1. Things I found that are about 1 meter long:

2. Things I found that are about 1 centimeter long:

Inches and Centimeters: Comparing Tools ✏️WRITING

Compare an inch ruler and a centimeter ruler.
Name 2 things that are the same.

1.

2.

Name 2 things that are different.

1.

2.

More Comparisons

Use a meterstick or the paper "meter strip" you made in school.

> **NOTE** Students investigate linear measurements and compare the length of objects.
>
> **SMH** 154

1. Find something that is **taller** than you are.

How tall is it? _____

2. How much taller than you is it? _____

3. Find something that is **wider** than your

shoulders. How wide is it? _____

4. How much wider than your shoulders is it? _____

5. Find something that is **shorter** than your foot.

How long is it? _____

6. How much shorter than your foot is it? _____

7. Find something that is **longer** than your pencil.

How long is it? _____

8. How much longer than your pencil is it? _____

Ongoing Review

9. You saved 75¢. Which 3 coupons did you use?

Ⓐ

Save 50¢	Save 25¢	Save 10¢

Ⓒ

Save 35¢	Save 25¢	Save 15¢

Ⓑ

Save 45¢	Save 25¢	Save 15¢

Ⓓ

Save 25¢	Save 25¢	Save 10¢

Metric Scavenger Hunt at Home

NOTE Students measure objects that are 1 meter long and 1 centimeter long.

SMH 154

Find things that are 1 meter long and 1 centimeter long.

1. Things I found that are about one meter long:

2. Things I found that are about one centimeter long:

© Pearson Education 2

Inches and Centimeters: Measuring ✏ WRITING

Measure each object. Record your measurements.

1. Your pencil is _____ inches long.

   Your pencil is _____ centimeters long.
   Circle the unit that gives you the larger number.

   inches   centimeters

2. Your book is _____ inches long.

   Your book is _____ centimeters long.
   Circle the unit that gives you the larger number.

   inches   centimeters

3. Your scissors are _____ inches long.

   Your scissors are _____ centimeters long.
   Circle the unit that gives you the larger number.

   inches   centimeters

4. Which unit always gives you the larger number?

   inches   centimeters

5. Why do you think this happens?

   _____

   _____

   _____

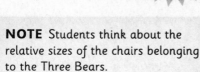

A Chair for Baby Bear

Baby Bear's chair broke. His parents decided to build him a new one.

NOTE Students think about the relative sizes of the chairs belonging to the Three Bears.

SMH **154**

The seat height of his old chair was 26 centimeters.

The seat height of his new chair needs to be 29 centimeters.

1. How much taller does the seat height of his new chair need to be?

_____ centimeters.

2. If the back of his new chair measures the same as the seat height, how tall will his new chair be? _____

3. If Mama Bear's chair is twice as tall as Baby Bear's new chair, how tall is it? _____

4. If Papa Bear's chair is twice as tall as Mama Bear's, how tall is it? _____

Ongoing Review

5. How far is it from 45 to 100?

Ⓐ 35   Ⓑ 45   Ⓒ 55   Ⓓ 65

At What Time? (page 1 of 2)

NOTE Students complete a timeline from a series of clues.

1. Michelle has lunch at 11:00 A.M.
Lunch lasts for 1 hour. Then it is time for
science. What time does science start? _____

2. School begins 3 hours before Michelle's
lunch period. What time does school begin? _____

3. After lunch, Michelle has science for half an hour,
then P.E. for 1 hour, and then another half an hour
of science. What time is it when science has ended
for the day? _____

4. The school day is 7 hours long.
What time does school end? _____

5. Right after school, Michelle has soccer practice
for $1\frac{1}{2}$ hours. Then she does her homework.
What time does Michelle start her homework? _____

At What Time? (page 2 of 2)

6. Show Michelle's day on the timeline.

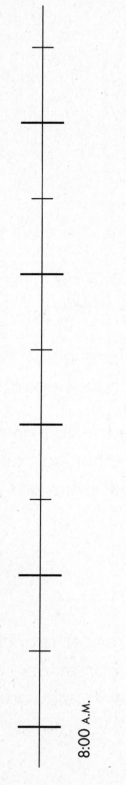

8:00 A.M.

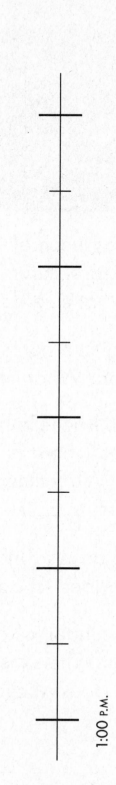

1:00 P.M.

Whose Foot Is It?

NOTE Students compare and describe measurements numerically, and find the shortest and longest.

1. Read the following clues.

- Pepe's foot is 2 centimeters shorter than Amy's foot.
- Rick's foot is the same length as Amy's foot.
- TJ's foot is 1 centimeter longer than Pepe's foot.
- Rosario's foot is longer than Amy's foot, but shorter than Ben's foot.
- Max's foot is the smallest of all!

2. Now write the person's name by the measurement that shows how long their foot is.

17 centimeters _____

18 centimeters _____

19 centimeters _____

20 centimeters _____

20 centimeters _____

21 centimeters _____

22 centimeters _____

Ongoing Review

3. What time is 3 hours after 9:00 A.M.?

(A) 1:30 P.M.

(B) 12:00 P.M.

(C) 11:00 A.M.

(D) 10:30 A.M.

Times for Morning and Evening Activities

For each activity, write the time it begins and ends.

NOTE Students write times for events that occur in their lives before and after school. Students will use this information in our next math class.

SMH 142

Before School

1. Wake up: Time: _____

2. Get ready for school: Begin: _____   End: _____
(including brushing your
teeth, getting dressed,
and eating breakfast)

3. Ride or walk to school: Begin: _____   End: _____

After School

4. Ride or walk home: Begin: _____   End: _____

5. Eat dinner: Begin: _____   End: _____

Write in any other activities you did.

6. Activity: _____   Begin: _____   End: _____

7. Activity: _____   Begin: _____   End: _____

Number Patterns

Complete the 100 chart.
Look for patterns.

NOTE Students use their knowledge of the counting sequence and patterns to fill in the missing numbers on a 100 chart.

SMH 24

100 Chart

	2	3	4		6	7	8	9	
11		13	14		16	17	18		20
21	22		24		26	27		29	30
31	32	33			36		38	39	40
						47	48	49	50
51	52	53	54						
61	62	63		65			68	69	70
71	72		74	75		77		79	80
81		83	84	85		87	88		90
	92	93	94	95		97	98	99	

A.M. and P.M.

For each time, write what you are usually doing.

NOTE Students work with the two 12-hour cycles of the 24-hour day.

SMH 142

7:00 A.M. _____

5:00 A.M. _____

12:00 P.M. (noon) _____

7:00 P.M. _____

5:00 P.M. _____

12:00 A.M. (midnight) _____

1. How many hours are there between
12:00 A.M. (midnight) and 12:00 P.M. (noon)?
Show how you figured it out.

2. Record the time the first clock shows. Make the
second clock show the same time for P.M. and
record the time.

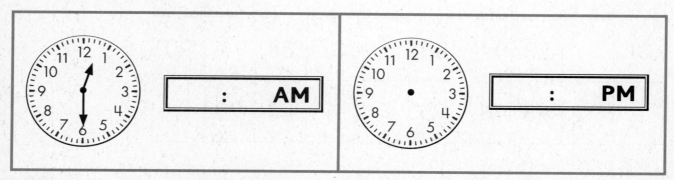

Fred & Winnipeg: Chapter 1

Winnipeg and Fred are two cats that live together in the city.

At **9:00** one morning, Winnipeg looked out the window and saw a flock of sparrows. "Yum," said Winnipeg. "I'd like a sparrow for breakfast." Fred opened one eye. "I'm too sleepy," Fred said. "OK," said Winnipeg. They went back to sleep for **1 hour.**

At **10:00** A.M., Winnipeg looked out the window and saw a pigeon. "Yum," said Winnipeg. "I'd like a pigeon for breakfast!" Fred again opened one eye. "I need a little nap," said Fred. "OK," said Winnipeg. So they went to sleep again for **2 more hours.**

When they woke up, Winnipeg looked out the window and saw a mouse. "Yum!" said Winnipeg. "I'm not waiting any longer! I want some lunch!" "OK," said Fred. So they went out hunting for mice until **1:00** P.M.

Then they curled up in the sun and went back to sleep for **1 hour.** Then they went home.

Fred & Winnipeg:
Chapter 1 Timeline

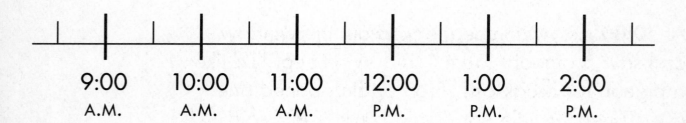

9:00	10:00	11:00	12:00	1:00	2:00
A.M.	A.M.	A.M.	P.M.	P.M.	P.M.

Fred & Winnipeg: Chapter 2

The next day, Winnipeg and Fred woke up at
8:00 A.M. Fred wanted to go back to sleep, but
Winnipeg said, "Oh no! Today, we're eating
breakfast right away. I'm hungry for a sparrow!"

They went out hunting for food for **2 hours.**
They came back and took a nap for **an hour
and a half.**

At **11:30 A.M.,** Winnipeg woke up. Winnipeg
said, "It's time for lunch." Fred said, "I know a
good place to get lunch. There's a lady who always
gives me cat food if I rub against her legs and purr."
So they started to walk. But Fred got lost. It took
them **half an hour** to walk to the lady's house.

The lady gave both cats food and milk. They stayed
at her house for **2 hours.**

At **2:00 P.M.** they began to walk home. Winnipeg
said, "I know a short cut." But they got lost again.
It took them **2 hours** to get home.

When they got home, Fred said, "I need a long
nap after all that walking." So they curled up
together in a box and went to sleep for **2 hours.** At
6:00 P.M., they woke up. Winnipeg said, "Oh good,
it's time for dinner!"

Fred & Winnipeg: Chapter 2 List of Events

To help you think about Fred and Winnipeg's day, use the following list of events and times.

Fill in the blanks for any missing times.

a. 8:00 A.M.   Fred and Winnipeg wake up.

b. 8:00 A.M. – _____   Go hunting for **2 hours**

c. _____ – 11:30 A.M.   Nap for **an hour and a half**

d. 11:30 A.M. – _____   Walk and get lost for **half an hour**

e. _____ – 2:00 P.M.   At lady's house for **2 hours**

f. 2:00 P.M. – _____   Walk home and get lost for **2 hours**

g. _____ – 6:00 P.M.   Nap for **2 hours**

Fred & Winnipeg: Chapter 2 Timeline

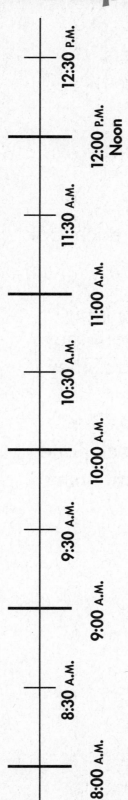

8:00 A.M.

8:30 A.M.

9:00 A.M.

9:30 A.M.

10:00 A.M.

10:30 A.M.

11:00 A.M.

11:30 A.M.

12:00 P.M.
Noon

12:30 P.M.

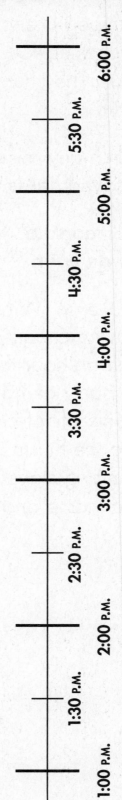

1:00 P.M.

1:30 P.M.

2:00 P.M.

2:30 P.M.

3:00 P.M.

3:30 P.M.

4:00 P.M.

4:30 P.M.

5:00 P.M.

5:30 P.M.

6:00 P.M.

Fred & Winnipeg: Chapter 3

Fred and Winnipeg like to go out together at night to hunt for mice. One night, they went out **at 10:00 P.M.** They hunted **for an hour and a half.**

They didn't catch any mice, so they went back home. They played cards **for 1 hour.**

At **12:30 A.M.,** Fred said, "I'm tired." They each took a nap **for half an hour.**

When they woke up, Winnipeg said, "My friend Cordelia is having a party tonight. Let's go!" They walked **for half an hour** to get to Cordelia's. They arrived at the party at **1:30 A.M.** It was a great party, with lots of cream and catnip. The cats danced to the music of the All Cat Rock Band. Fred and Winnipeg stayed **for 2 and a half hours.** Then they went home and went to sleep.

Fred & Winnipeg:
Chapter 3 List of Events

To help you think about Fred and Winnipeg's day, use the following list of events and times.

Fill in the blanks for any missing times.

a. 10:00 P.M.   Fred and Winnipeg went out.

b. 10:00 P.M. – _____   Went hunting for **an hour and a half**

c. _____ – 12:30 A.M.   Played cards for **1 hour**

d. 12:30 A.M.   Fred said, "I'm tired."

e. 12:30 A.M. – _____   Napped for **half an hour**

f. _____ – 1:30 A.M.   Walked to Cordelia's for **half an hour**

g. 1:30 A.M. – _____   At party for **two and a half hours**

h. 4:00 A.M.   Went home

Fred & Winnipeg: Chapter 3 Timeline

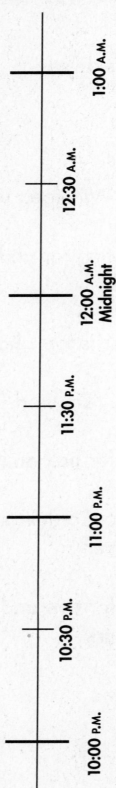

1:00 A.M.

12:30 A.M.

12:00 A.M.
Midnight

11:30 P.M.

11:00 P.M.

10:30 P.M.

10:00 P.M.

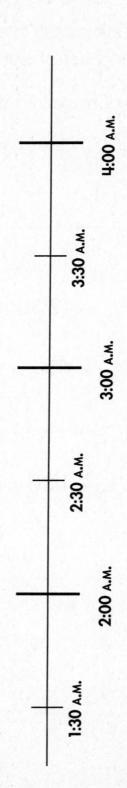

4:00 A.M.

3:30 A.M.

3:00 A.M.

2:30 A.M.

2:00 A.M.

1:30 A.M.

What Is Going on Today?

NOTE Students create a timeline and show duration of activities on it.

SMH **143, 144, 145**

© Pearson Education 2

Create a timeline. Use **all** of the required activities. Choose **two** of the special activities. Show how long each special activity lasts.

Required Activities
Waking up at 7:00 A.M.
Breakfast at 8:00 A.M.
Lunch at 12:00 P.M.
Dinner at 6:00 P.M.
Going to bed at 9:00 P.M.

Special Activities
Swimming at 9:00 A.M. for 2 hours
Library at 10:00 A.M. for 1 hour
Movie at 1:00 P.M. for 2 hours
Park at 3:00 P.M. for 1 hour
Baseball at 5:00 P.M. for 1 hour

7:00 A.M. | 8:00 A.M. | 9:00 A.M. | 10:00 A.M. | 11:00 A.M. | 12:00 NOON | 1:00 P.M. | 2:00 P.M. | 3:00 P.M. | 4:00 P.M. | 5:00 P.M. | 6:00 P.M. | 7:00 P.M. | 8:00 P.M. | 9:00 P.M.

Fred & Winnipeg Timeline Problems (page 1 of 2)

Look at the timeline.

How long did each activity take?

Activity	Begins	Ends	How long did it take?
Eating Breakfast	10:00	11:00	1 hour
Chasing Mice			
Taking Bath			
First Nap			
Visiting Lili			
Second Nap			
Eating Dinner			
Third Nap			
Meowing at Moon			
Sleeping			

Fred & Winnipeg
Timeline Problems (page 2 of 2)

1. After breakfast, Fred said, "How long until dinner?"

How long did Fred have to wait for dinner? _____

How did you figure it out? _____

_____

_____

2. When they got up, Winnipeg said, "I wonder when Lili will get here?" How long did Winnipeg have to wait for Lili? _____

How did you figure it out? _____

_____

_____

3. How long did Fred and Winnipeg sleep? Include all of the times they were asleep or napping. _____

How did you figure it out? _____

_____

_____

How Long Does It Take?

Circle the activity that takes the shorter amount of time.

NOTE Students compare the duration of two activities and determine which activity takes less or more time.

SMH 145

1.

Brushing teeth   Eating breakfast

2.

Sleeping at night   Getting dressed

Circle the activity that takes the longer amount of time.

3.

Eating an ice cream cone   Playing a baseball game

4.

Watching a movie   Blowing up a balloon

Special Day Activities

Think of activities you would like to do at different times of the day.

You will choose some activities to make a Special Day Timeline tomorrow, so it is important that this assignment be completed and returned to school.

NOTE Students write events that could occur in their lives on a special day. They will use these events to make a Special Day Timeline in our next math class.

SMH 143

Morning Activities:

_____   _____

_____   _____

Afternoon Activities:

_____   _____

_____   _____

Evening Activities:

_____   _____

_____   _____

Night Activities:

_____   _____

_____   _____

Fraction Flags

Write what fraction of the flag each color is.

NOTE Students use what they know about fractions to determine how much of a flag is shaded a certain color.

SMH **84, 85, 86, 87**

1. Black: _____

   White: _____

2. Gray: _____

   White: _____

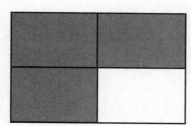

3. Gray: _____

   White: _____

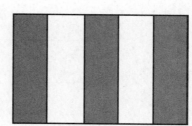

4. Black: _____

   White: _____

5. Black: _____

   White: _____

   Gray: _____

Comparing Special Day Timelines

Use the Special Day Timelines from our class to answer these questions.

1. Who got up the earliest? _____

What time? _____

2. Who woke up the latest? _____

What time? _____

3. Who did one activity
for a very long time? _____

What was the activity? _____

How long was it? _____

4. Who did something for exactly
1 hour and a half?

Who did it? _____

What was the activity? _____

What time did it start? _____

What time did it end? _____

How Many More?

Kira has 57 dog stickers.
Jake has 70 dog stickers.

NOTE Students use addition or subtraction to find the difference between two quantities.

SMH 73–75

How many more dog stickers
does Jake have than Kira?

Solve the problem. Show your work.
Write an equation.

me?

1. Michelle has lunch at 11:00 A.M. Lunch lasts for 1 hour. Then it is time for science. What time does science start? _____

2. School begins 3 hours before Michelle's lunch period. What time does school begin? _____

3. After lunch, Michelle has science for half an hour, then P.E. for 1 hour, and then another half hour of science. What time is it when science ends? _____

4. The school day is 7 hours long. What time does school end? _____

5. Right after school, Michelle has soccer practice for $1\frac{1}{2}$ hours. Then she does her homework. What time does Michelle start her homework? _____

Now, on a separate sheet of paper, make a timeline that shows Michelle's day. Start your timeline at 7:00 A.M. Be sure to include the information from each clue.